My Way
Or
Thy Way

A Book Of
"Choice" Bible Skits

Pat Betteley

CSS Publishing Company, Inc., Lima, Ohio

MY WAY OR THY WAY

For more information about CSS Publishing Company resources, visit our website at www.csspub.com or e-mail us at custserv@csspub.com or call (800) 241-4056.

ISBN 0-7880-2313-6

PRINTED IN U.S.A.

For Adam who bit, and Noah who built;
For Jacob who schemed, and Joseph who dreamed;
For Moses who led, and Ruth who followed

For Solomon the king, and Esther the queen;
For Peter who lied, and Jesus who died;
For ordinary people faced with extraordinary choices ...

Table Of Contents

*All skits in this book are based on
the New International Version of the Bible.*

Introduction

To My Readers:
"And then he looked straight at me. I thought I'd die."
"I would have. Right then and there. What a *major* disaster!"
Ever overhear a preteen or early teen conversation? Pretty dramatic. In fact, young people and drama go together like ... God and the Bible. This book of plays is designed to draw ages ten through adult into Bible stories by using contemporary conversation that is easy to understand. Drama helps youth/adults understand stories more intensely than just reading about lifeless historical characters — and gives them memories to last a lifetime. After each skit, lively discussion questions are provided that focus on choices made by the main characters and their consequences. These and other related activities help children apply Bible truths to their own lives.

The skits are designed for versatility. A teacher, youth leader, director, or worship coordinator can choose skits to enhance existing curriculum, and simply have students read through their parts and skip the production notes. Or any of the skits can be presented as a full-blown play with props, scenery, and costumes.

Dramatically inclined leaders may want to plan an entire year's curriculum using one skit per month, and covering Bible history from Adam and Eve through Jesus. A chart such as the one that follows can be put on a chalkboard, bulletin board, poster board, or large piece of paper and used for comparison, contrast, and review throughout the Bible study.

	Bible Character(s)	Choice(s)	Consequence(s)	Message Learned from his/her life
Example:	Adam	Ate the forbidden fruit	Kicked out of Garden of Eden	Obey God. Don't be influenced by others.

So to all who use this resource: I wish you laughter, increased confidence, a new camaraderie with your friends, fresh motivation to attend church or youth group, and a deeper understanding of God's plan in your own life.

May you feast on the banquet of Bible stories, eat and drink with the men and women who shaped our Christian heritage, and for dessert, share their stories with others. Bon apétit!

Yours in Christian Theater,
Pat Betteley

Adam And Eve:
The First Couple

A play based on Genesis 1-3

This play is dual purpose. It can be used in the classroom as a "Reader's Theater" piece to spark discussion, or it can be presented in the sanctuary with a few basic props.

Scene: The play is in one act. The scene is the Garden of Eden. The Narrator speaks from the lectern or stage left. The Tree of the Knowledge of Good and Evil is center stage. The Tree of Life is right stage. (Optional Angel stands in front of it at appropriate time in script.) All action takes place center stage, except that God snoozes right stage or in front of steps if stage has two levels.

Props: Optional stuffed animals and toy box, the Tree of the Knowledge of Good and Evil and the Tree of Life (could be painted cardboard, fig trees, or inflatable palms available at party supply stores), lawn chair, optional stuffed lion and tiger (younger children can be used, instead), apple, play sword

Sound Effects: (Optional) Sneaky piano melody to be played as Snake enters and exits

Characters:
Narrator — reader
God — the Creator
Adam — first man created by God
Lion — (optional) young child who growls like lion
Tiger — (optional) young child who bares claws like tiger
Snake — Satan in disguise
Woman — Eve, first woman created by God
Angel — (optional) fiercely defends Tree of Life

9

Time: the beginning of time.

Costumes: Street clothes for Narrator; neutral colored sweatsuits for Adam and Eve, green paper fig leaf that ties around waist for Adam when script calls for it, two vests to be put on at end of skit; white robe and sun visor for God; Halloween costumes or simple paper ears and face make-up can be used for optional Lion and Tiger; Snake could be a hand puppet with the actor/actress wearing khaki pants, hiking boots, and explorer's hat; robe, wings, halo for optional Angel

---

Narrator: On the sixth day of creation, God made all the animals. *(Pulls stuffed animals out of toy box and arranges by tree)* Then God picked up some dust from the ground and formed a man, breathing life into his nostrils. *(God stands by tree and pantomimes picking up dust, shaping it, breathing life into it)* This man was called Adam. *(Adam steps out from behind tree)* God put him in charge of all the fish, birds, animals, and plants in the Garden of Eden.

God: *(To Adam)* Help yourself to anything in the fridge — er, I mean garden. You may eat from any tree except that one in the middle called the Tree of the Knowledge of Good and Evil. If you eat from that one, you'll die.

Adam: The first rule. Sounds fair enough to me. Now, to name all my little critter-friends. Let's see, *(Picking up stuffed lion)* you can be a tion, and you, *(Picking up tiger)* liger. No, let's switch that around. You're lion, and you're tiger. That's better. Whew, this is harder than it looks. Wish I had someone to help me.

Narrator: God saw that Adam was lonely, so he made him fall fast asleep. *(God passes hand in front of Adam's eyes. Adam curls up and sleeps)* While he was snoozing, God took one of the man's ribs and made it into a woman. *(God pretends to take rib and form it. Woman steps out from behind tree)*

10

Adam: She is bone of my bones and flesh of my flesh. I'll call her Wo-man because she was taken out of man.

Narrator: On the seventh day, God was pooped.

God: Just look at those two innocents. They're so happy, they don't even know they're naked. Yes, everything I've made is *very* good, but I've worked hard for six days. I think I'll take a well-deserved rest. *(Sinks back into lawn chair and pulls sun visor over his eyes)*

Narrator: Meanwhile, back in the garden, Adam and his Woman were meeting their neighbors. Little did they know that the crafty Snake was really Satan in disguise trying to tempt them.

Snake: *(Enters through side door. Piano can play melody line of sneaky music, if desired)* Did God s-s-s-s-s-say that you couldn't eat from any tree in the garden?

Woman: No, we can eat from all of them, except that one right in the middle. *(Points toward Tree of the Knowledge of Good and Evil)* If we touch it, we'll die.

Snake: S-s-s-s-s-urely you don't believe everything that control freak tells you? You won't die if you eat from it. In fact, your eyes will be opened and you'll be like God, knowing right from wrong.

Woman: Really? Well, I *am* a little hungry, and that fruit *would* make a tasty snack. *(Picks fruit from tree)*

Snake: Of course it would. S-s-s-s-s-ink your teeth right in ...

Woman: *(Bites into fruit)* Yum! Tastes great. Here, Adam. Try a bite.

Adam: *(Bites into fruit)* M-m-m-m-m, good. *(Swallows with a ...)* Glunk!

11

Snake: Look, a chunk is s-s-s-s-s-s-stuck in your throat. That must be your Adam's apple!

Adam: Very funny. Br-r-r-r-. I'm chilly. *(To Eve)* Are you?

Woman: Now that you mention it, yes. *(Adam and Woman look at each other and gasp, realizing they're both naked. They look embarrassed)* Excuse us for a minute while I do some sewing. *(Both turn their backs and Adam ties on fig leaf)* There we go — the first underwear!

Narrator: When God woke up from his nap, he took a walk in the garden. *(God wakes up, stretches and walks through audience to get back to garden)* Adam and his wife heard him and hid. *(Adam and Woman hide behind tree)*

God: Where are you?

Adam: *(From behind tree)* There's nobody here but us fig trees.

God: Why are you hiding?

Adam: Er, hiding? Um, because we're both ... naked. *(Adam and Woman step out from behind tree trying to cover themselves)*

God: Who told you that? Did you eat from the Tree of the Knowledge of Good and Evil? The one I told you to stay away from?

Woman: *(Nodding yes and pinching a "tiny bit" with her thumb and forefinger)* Just an ever-so-tiny bite.

Adam: She gave it to me, so I ate it.

God: What have you done?

Woman: The snake told me to do it.

God: Curse you, serpent. Because you have done this, you will crawl on your belly and eat dust for the rest of your days. And you and all of Eve's children will hate each other — them crushing your head, and you biting their heels.

Snake: That seems harsh-sh-sh-sh. *(Gets down on belly and slithers away. Optional sneaky melody)*

God: And you, Woman. Because you listened to him, having babies is going to hurt — a lot, and your husband will rule over you.

Adam: Sounds fair to me. The husband-ruler part, I mean.

God: Adam, I am most disappointed in you. Because you disobeyed, I now curse the ground you walk on. It will produce thorns and thistles, and you'll have to do back-breaking, sweaty work to get any food from it. When you die, you'll turn back into the dust you were made from.

Narrator: Adam then named his wife Eve, because she would be the mother of all the living. And God made them clothes to wear. *(God gives each a vest to put on)* But God worried that they would eat from the Tree of Life and live forever like him.

God: You must leave the Garden of Eden forever. I'm leaving a mighty angel with a flaming sword to guard the Tree of Life so that you can never return. *(Angel appears, waving sword in "z" stroke)*

Narrator: And so the first couple whose children's children are our great-great, ever-so-great, great-grandparents, sadly trudged away from their perfect Garden of Eden, learning the hard way that one should always obey God. *(Adam and Eve lower heads in shame and drag feet as they walk out down center aisle of audience)*

Discussion Questions

1. Why is it hard to recognize Satan in this skit? Why is it hard to recognize Satan in our lives today?

2. How do you know whether something you want to do is right or wrong?

3. What poor choice did Adam and Eve make?

4. What were the consequences of their choice?

5. Do you think God's consequences were fair? Why / why not?

Related Activities

1. Have students create (and name) their own animals using clay, feathers, movable eyes, pipe cleaners, etc.

2. Have students paint trees on cardboard for use in the play. These are great basic pieces that can be used for future productions.

3. Students can make headpieces (ears) for lion and tiger.

4. Make a big chart/poster that has lots of room to grow. Write four categories across the top: Bible Character(s), Choice(s), Consequence(s), Message Learned from His/Her Life. Fill the chart in for the Adam and Eve story.

5. Present the skit for younger children.
   a. Afterwards, let them role play different animals that God might have created in the Garden of Eden, while everyone guesses which animal they're acting out.
   b. Sing "He's got the _____ and the _____ in his hands," to the tune of "He's Got The Whole World In His Hands," with the younger children, letting them choose different animals to fill in the blanks.

Noah And The Flood

A play based on Genesis 6:5—9:17

This play is designed to be read and discussed with no props or scenery or produced as a simple one-act play with minimal effects. The ideal performance area would have two levels connected by stairs.

Scenes: Action is continuous on center stage, with Stage Crew, characters moving props on and off as per the script. Narrator stands at lectern or offstage with microphone. God stands higher than Noah, on a platform, chair, or in the choirloft.

Props: two folding lawn chairs, two cans of pop, three white beards, twelve stuffed animals (bean bag animals work well, preferably two of each of six kinds), ark painted on cardboard with two sticks horizontally on either side to be held by Stage Crew, hammer, carpenter's measuring tape, paint brush, optional blue sheet for water to be held by two Stage Crew members, cardboard rainbow on two vertical sticks to be held up by two Stage Crew members

Characters:
Narrator — reader
Noah — God's faithful servant
God — the Almighty
Neighbor 1 — doubting townsperson
Neighbor 2 — another doubter
Stage Crew — two to hold ark, two to hold rainbow and optional
    sheet, non-speaking
Shem — Noah's son, non-speaking, optional
Ham — Noah's son, non-speaking, optional
Japheth — Noah's son, non-speaking, optional

15

Wife 1 — married to Shem, non-speaking, optional
Wife 2 — married to Ham, non-speaking, optional
Wife 3 — married to Japheth, non-speaking, optional

Time: undated — before 2000 B.C.

Costumes: Noah, two Neighbors, Shem, Ham, Japheth, and Wives wear biblical robes with scarves covering heads, rope belts, and sandals. God wears flowing white robe. Narrator and Stage Crew wear regular clothes

---

Narrator: This is the story of a man who lived through not one, but two floods in his 950-year lifetime. The first one was a flood of evil. Ever since the Garden of Eden, people's attitudes kept getting worse until there was only one man left on the whole earth who still worshiped God. His name was Noah.

Noah: *(Walks center stage)* Good morning, God. Thank you for another beautiful day.

God: *(From above)* And thank you for your positive attitude. Unfortunately, you're the only one left who isn't evil.

Narrator: Here's where the second flood I mentioned comes in ...

God: I'm going to flood the earth and destroy every breathing creature except for those of you on the ark that you are going to build. Here's where you come in ... Make yourself a boat of cypress wood the length of one and a half football fields and as high as a four-story building with three decks. I promise that you, your wife, your three sons, and their wives will be spared along with the animals on board.

Noah: Animals, sir?

God: Yes. You are to bring two of each kind of living creature on earth aboard with you — one male and one female.

Noah: As in birds, and four-footed critters, and even slimy things that go slither in the night?

God: Exactly.

Noah: Mrs. Noah's going to love this. But you NO-AH me, God; I'll do as you say. I can be a very patient, man.

God: I *know-uh.*

Narrator: And Noah did everything as God had commanded, building his ark on dry land. His neighbors thought he was more cracked than the timbers he coated with water-proof pitch. *(Stage Crew brings in ark. Noah pretends to pound with hammer)*

Neighbor 1: *(Neighbors enter with fold-up lawn chairs and cans of pop)* Hey, Noah. Have you seen the weather forecast?

Neighbor 2: Dry and sunny again. Guess that kind of knocks out your God's death and destruction plan. *(Both Neighbors laugh, set up lawn chairs, drink pop, and watch)*

Noah: God's plans unfold in God's own time.

Narrator: And time marched on. *(Noah pretends to measure ark with measuring tape. Optional effect, Noah and two Neighbors put on white beards)*

Noah: *(Puts final stroke on ark with paintbrush)* Whew! Building this monstrous ark has taken 120 years, but my patience has finally paid off. The ark is finished!

17

God: Good job, Noah. Now take your wife, your sons, Shem, Ham, and Japheth, and their wives, and a male and female of every kind of animal and bird on earth and board the ark. In seven days, I'll send the rain which will last for forty days and nights. It will wipe out every living creature from the face of the earth.

Neighbor 1: *(Sticks hand out to feel rain)* What's that? I feel a raindrop.

Neighbor 2: It's not supposed to rain today. You don't think that ... Nah. *(Neighbors fold up lawn chairs and exit quickly, trying to cover heads from rain)*

Narrator: So, Noah, his family, and about 45,000 animals entered the ark. *(Noah, optional Mrs. Noah, Shem, Ham, Japheth, three Wives enter, each carrying stuffed animals which they hang over edges and in windows of ark. All stand behind ark with heads showing)* Just as God had said, it rained for forty days and the waters covered even the highest mountains by at least twenty feet. While the ark floated gently, every living thing on dry land was wiped out. *(Optional effect — two Stage Crew make blue sheet billow low in front of ark like water while two Stage Crew move ark up and down with sticks as if rocking on waves)*

Noah: *(Standing on deck of ark)* God, I'm 600 years old, and I think I've shown I'm a pretty patient guy, but if the floods haven't killed everyone on earth by now, the smell of our ark will!

Narrator: After the earth has been flooded for 150 days, God sent a wind to dry things up. The water level went down until the ark came to rest on the mountains of Ararat.

Noah: Let me open a window. *(Pantomimes opening window. Takes deep breath)* Ah — fresh air. Let's see if the dove can find dry land.

Narrator: The dove could find no place to land, so it flew back to Noah, who waited seven more days and sent it out again. This time, it came back with a fresh olive leaf in its beak. The third time Noah sent it out, the dove never returned at all. *(Stage Crew lays down blue sheet and exits)*

God: Noah, time to disem-*bark*, and *meow* and *whinny* and *chirp*.

Noah: What?

God: Get off the boat!

Narrator: So Noah with his family and all the creatures filed out of the ark — one kind after the other. *(All leave ark and stand in front of it, center stage)*

Noah: *(Kneels in prayer)* God, you are so good. Thank you for delivering us safely.

God: May you and your family and all of these creatures be fruitful and multiply.

Noah: I'm not much for fruit, and my math skills are definitely weak.

God: No, Noah. What I mean is — have babies!

Noah: Oh.

Narrator: And then God made a beautiful rainbow in the clouds. *(Two Stage Crew members enter with rainbow and hold it up over cast, center stage)*

God: Let this rainbow be a sign of my promise to you: I will never again make a flood which destroys the whole earth, the seasons will always come and go, and the rainbow after the rain will remind you that I keep my promises.

Narrator: And Noah's son's sons spread out over the earth after the flood, forming many nations who spoke many languages. *(Three Sons and Wives exit, each going down a different aisle, waving)* As for Noah, he faithfully obeyed God his whole life and was definitely fruitful — living to the *ripe* old age of 950!

Discussion Questions

1. Why did God want to destroy the world?

2. What choice could Noah have made when his neighbors mocked him for building an ark on dry land? What were the consequences of the choice he made?

3. Patient. Obedient. Faithful. Grateful. Tell how each of these applies to Noah.

4. The neighbors watched Noah build the ark for 120 years. What do you think God would have done if the neighbors had begun to worship him again during those long years?

5. What symbolized God's pledge never to flood the entire earth again?

Related Activities

1. Make props for the play:
   a. Ark: sketch on big piece of cardboard according to description in play or Genesis 6:16. Include round portholes. Reinforce back with yardsticks, wood strips taped to cardboard. Extend poles horizontally from each side for crew to carry ark. Paint and cut out.
   b. Sketch, paint, and cut out rainbow on cardboard and hold up with vertical poles taped to back. Alternate idea: Give each cast member material, scarf, or paper of a different color and let them hold these up when the narrator mentions the rainbow.

2. Use your math skills to figure out how long Noah was on the ark, using the following passages: Genesis 7:24, Genesis 8:6, Genesis 8:10, Genesis 8:12.

3. Visit the preschool/kindergarten classroom. Perform the skit for them. Take turns pantomiming animals for them to guess, then let them pantomime for you. Sing "The Arky Song" from *Wee Sing Bible Songs* (by Beall and Nipp, Price/Stern/Sloan, 1986) with them. Read *Why Noah Chose the Dove* (Isaac Bashevis Singer) to them, and serve animal crackers for a snack.

4. Look up other versions of great floods in history and compare them to the story of Noah using a Venn Diagram (see below).

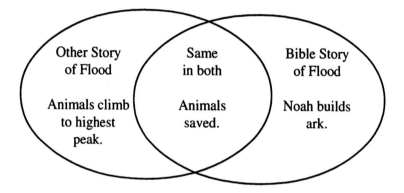

List events that happened only in the Bible version of the flood in the oval on the right, events that happened only in the other version in the oval on the left, and events common to both versions in the center where the ovals intersect.

Some resources are:
Ellen Alexander, *Llama and the Great Flood: A Folktale from Peru* (New York: Thomas Y. Crowell, 1989).
Emery Bernhard, *The Tree That Rains: The Flood Myth of the Huichol Indians of Mexico* (New York: Holiday House, 1994).

Pauline E. Johnson, "The Deep Waters" (Squamish flood myth from British Columbia in Canada), *Legends of Vancouver* (Vancouver: Douglas and McIntyre, 1997).

Brian Wildsmith, *Professor Noah's Spaceship* (Oxford: Oxford University Press, 1980).

5. Add Noah's name to your chart of Bible Character(s), Choice(s), Consequence(s), and Message Learned.

Jacob And Esau: Trickery In The Genes

A play based on Genesis 25-29

This play is designed to be read and discussed with no scenery, or produced easily with a few simple props. It is in one act, though the action occurs continuously over time. A sanctuary or auditorium with stairs or different levels would work best for production.

Scenes: All scenes take place in front of Isaac and Rebekah's tent. A rustic table and chair sit center stage. At lower level (bottom of steps) are some logs stacked to look like a campfire. A picnic basket sits right stage. Narrator stands at lectern, left stage. God stands at higher level, such as top step, platform, or choir left.

Props: Rustic table and chair; logs arranged like campfire; picnic basket; animal skin for Esau's costume. Optional props: bow and quiver of arrows, fake beard, cane, pillow, stuffed pillow case or burlap bag (to hold goats), fake fur strips to cover neck/hands, tape

Characters:
Narrator — reader
God — the Creator
Isaac — son of Abraham, husband of Rebekah, father of Jacob and Esau
Rebekah — married to Isaac, meddling mom
Esau — firstborn twin
Jacob — secondborn twin

23

Time: 2006-1929 B.C.

Costumes: Regular modern clothing for Narrator; white robe for God; biblical garb for Jacob and Isaac (Isaac adds optional fake beard and cane after he ages); biblical robe for Esau with animal skin laying over one shoulder and optional bow and quiver of arrows slung over other shoulder, optional leather strips tied from sandals up to knee; biblical robe for Rebekah, optional belt with a pillow underneath for first scene

---

Narrator: Isaac was afraid that his wife, Rebekah, would never have any children, so he prayed to the Lord. *(Isaac center stage, kneels in prayer)* His prayers were answered when he found out that his wife would be having twins. *(Rebekah enters, very pregnant)*

Rebekah: *(With her hand on optional pillow or stomach)* But why do they jostle each other so much inside my belly?

God: Two nations are in your womb,
  You will give birth to two separate nations;
  One people will be stronger than the other,
  And the older will serve the younger.

Narrator: Talk about your recipe for sibling rivalry! Anyway, the first twin born was Esau, which means "hairy." Next, holding on to his brother's foot, came Jacob, which means "he grasps the heel" or "he deceives." When the boys grew up, Esau became a skillful hunter, loved best by his father. *(Esau enters. Father Isaac puts hand on shoulder affectionately or they do a secret handshake)*
  Jacob was quiet and stayed among the tents. He was loved best by his mother. *(Jacob enters and Rebekah pinches his cheek)* One day, Jacob was cooking some stew. *(Jacob walks down steps and sits at campfire, stirring pretend pot of stew. Isaac and Rebekah*

24

freeze. Esau pretends to see some game, and sneaks off down an aisle to track game. He draws optional bow, then continues around the pews and back to the campfire where Jacob is sitting, humming "We Are Climbing Jacob's Ladder" and stirring the stew) Soon, brother Esau, came in from the open country a long day of hunting.

Esau: I'm starving. Quick, give me some of that red stew.

Jacob: Sure, if you'll sell me your birthright.

Esau: Birthright? I'm ready to keel over any minute now, and you're worried about my birthright?

Jacob: Swear to me that it's mine.

Esau: Okay, I swear. What good is a birthright to a dead man! *(Jacob gives him an imaginary bowl of stew, which he wolfs down hungrily, then wipes his mouth on his arm)*

Narrator: *(Isaac puts on fake beard, bends down over cane. Rebekah moves off to side stage)* So Esau gave up his birthright for some lentil stew. Alas, that would not be the last trickery in the family. When Isaac became so old that he could no longer see, he called for Esau. *(Esau walks up steps and stands center stage next to Isaac. Rebekah cups hand over ear and leans toward them, eavesdropping)*

Isaac: Esau, I am ready to die. Before I go, I want to give you my blessing. So, go out to the open country, hunt some wild game for me, prepare it, and bring it for me to eat. Then I will bless you, my oldest son!

Narrator: Rebekah had been listening and called her favorite son to her.

Rebekah: *(Motions Jacob over to her side stage. Jacob walks over)* Jacob, your father will soon give his blessing to Esau. Listen, carefully, for I want you to receive that blessing. Bring me two choice young goats from the flock. I'll make his favorite dish, and you serve it to him, pretending to be Esau so you'll get his blessing.

Jacob: But, Mother, Esau is a hairy man, and I'm smooth-skinned. If father touches me, he'll know that I'm trying to trick him, and curse me instead.

Rebekah: Not to worry. Just get the goats. I'll take care of the rest. *(Jacob walks down steps and around block of pew, picking up a stuffed sack along the way, which he takes back to Rebekah at right stage)*

Narrator: So Jacob brought the goats to his mother who prepared them to perfection. *(Jacob hands Rebekah optional stuffed bag. Optional sound effect: cast makes bleating noise like goats)* Then she took Esau's best clothes and put them on Jacob. *(Lays Esau's animal skin robe over Jacob's shoulder)* She covered his hands and neck with goatskins and told him to take the food to Isaac. *(Rebekah places optional fake fur on his hands and neck, taping them if necessary. Gives him picnic basket, and gently pushes him toward Jacob, center stage, who is sitting stooped over in chair by table)*

Jacob: Father, here I am.

Isaac: Who?

Jacob: Esau — your firstborn.

Narrator: *Big* fib.

Jacob: Please sit up and eat, then give me your blessing.

26

Isaac: But, how did you hunt the game so quickly?

Jacob: The Lord gave me success.

Narrator: Half-truth.

Isaac: Not so fast, son. Come over here. I want to touch you to make sure that you're really Esau. *(Jacob stands next to Isaac who feels the fake fur on his hands)* H-m-m-m-m-m. You have Jacob's voice, but Esau's hands. Are you really my son Esau?

Jacob: I am.

Narrator: *Huge lie!*

Isaac: Then bring me my food, and I will give you my blessing. *(Jacob pretends to unpack picnic basket on table. Feeds his father imaginary food with a fork)* Yum, delicious ...
　　You smell of the field that the Lord has blessed.
　　May God give you an abundance of grain and wine.
　　May nations serve you.
　　May you be lord over your brothers.
　　May those who curse you be cursed
　　And those who bless you be blessed.

Jacob: Thank you, Father. *(Exits left stage with picnic basket. Passes it to Esau who is entering)*

Narrator: No sooner than Jacob had left, Esau arrived on the scene with some tasty food for his father.

Esau: *(Stands next to his father's chair, setting picnic basket back on table)* Father, I've brought your favorite meal for you to eat. Then you can give me your blessing.

Isaac: Who are you?

Esau: Your firstborn son, Esau.

Isaac: Then who was it that I just blessed? And indeed, he will be blessed. *(Shakes head sadly and jabs his cane on ground)* Your brother, Jacob, tricked me — and took your blessing.

Esau: That's the second time. First he took my birthright, and now my blessing. Haven't you any blessing left for me, father?

Jacob: *(Rises unsteadily, leaning heavily on cane)* I'll do the best I can, my son ...
    You will live away from the earth's riches.
    You will live by the sword and serve your brother,
    But when you get restless,
    You'll throw off his yoke.

Narrator: Esau was furious. He held a grudge against his brother, Jacob, and planned to seek his revenge.

Esau: *(Walks down steps by campfire, pounding fist into hand)* I'm going to kill that guy! *(Freezes in that pose)*

Narrator: *(Rebekah stands right stage with her hand to her ear, eavesdropping again)* Once again, big-eared Rebekah heard of Esau's plan, and sent Jacob to live with her brother, Laban, in Paddan Aram. *(Jacob enters, walks behind Esau to his mother, right stage)*

Rebekah: You must go now, son. Fortunately, it's time for you to choose a bride, anyway. And I don't want you to get stuck with any of the pushy Canaanite women from around here. Maybe while you're at my brother's you could find yourself a nice Jewish girl to marry, eh? *(Gently pushes him toward center aisle, which he walks down, exiting out back door)*

Narrator: So Jacob went to stay with his relatives, where he *did* find a nice Jewish girl to marry, just as his mother had wished.

Her name was Rachel, and she was the daughter of his Uncle Laban. Unfortunately, trickery ran in Rebekah's family, for her brother, Laban, tricked Jacob into marrying his other daughter, Leah instead.

Esau: Na-na, na-na, na! *(Sticks out tongue and makes face at back door)*

Narrator: And some would say it served him right.

Discussion Questions

1. What choices did Jacob make in this story? What choices did Esau make? What were the consequences of their choices?

2. Esau became the father of a weak nation called Edom. Jacob was the father of Israel, whose descendants include Moses, David, John the Baptist, and Jesus. How do these facts relate to God's prediction to Rebekah at the beginning of the play?

3. How would you feel if your brother tricked you, as Jacob did Esau? What would you do about it?

4. Should birthrights and blessings be more important than they are in today's society? Why or why not?

Related Activities

1. Look up the story of how the trickster was tricked in Genesis 29:15-30. Discuss how patience was rewarded in Jacob's case. Write your own skit about how Joseph was tricked and perform it for the younger children.

2. Read Genesis 33:1-5 to see if Esau held a grudge against Jacob as an adult. Do you think your own family disagreements might be forgiven in time?

3. Read about Jacob's dream in Genesis 28:12-14. This is the passage from which the song "We Are Climbing Jacob's Ladder," was taken. What does the ladder in his dream connect? Sing the song together.

4. Jacob's parents had obvious favorite children as he grew up, which caused some problems for the family. Did Jacob learn his lesson, and make sure not to show favoritism in his own family? Read the story of Joseph, his son, in Genesis 37:1-4 to find out. Listen to a tape or CD of *Joseph and the Amazing Technicolor Dreamcoat*, by Andrew Lloyd Webber.

5. Add Jacob's and Esau's names to your Choice Chart of Bible Character(s), their Choice(s), Consequence(s), and Message Learned.

Joseph And His Brothers

A play based on Genesis 37-47

Although there are several different scenes in this skit, for simplicity's sake it can be performed in one continuous act, with the scenes located in different areas of the stage or altar area.

Scenes: Canaan (center stage in front of steps), Potiphar's house in Egypt (center stage), prison (right stage), Pharaoh's palace in Egypt (center stage, same as Potiphar's). Narrator stands at lectern or offstage with microphone. Jacob is on stage as scene opens.

Props: Multi-colored robe

Characters:
Narrator — reader
Jacob — Father of twelve sons
Reuben — Jacob's son
Simeon — Jacob's son
Joseph — Jacob's son
Dan — Jacob's son
Gad — Jacob's son
Asher — Jacob's son
Ishmaelites — a foreign tribe, non-speaking
Potiphar — Pharaoh's Captain of the Guard
Cupbearer — prisoner in jail with Joseph
Baker — prisoner in jail with Joseph
Pharaoh — ruler of Egypt

Time: 1915-1885 B.C.

Costumes: Bible garb for Jacob, Reuben, Simeon, Joseph, Dan, Gad, Asher, Ishmaelites, Cupbearer; additional multi-colored robe and royal robe for Joseph; Egyptian robe, sword for Potiphar; white robe and chef's hat for Baker; royal robe and crown for Pharaoh

---

Narrator: Long ago, before men and women realized that it was a bad idea to show favoritism, a man named Jacob lived in the land of Canaan with his wife, Rachel, and their twelve sons.

Jacob: *(Joseph enters)* Ah, Joseph, favorite son of my favorite wife, Rachel. How can an old man help spoiling the child of his old age?

Joseph: *(Out of breath)* Father, my brothers are being lazy again. I'm the only one that does any sheep-tending around here.

Jacob: Those older boys like to give you a hard time, don't they, son? Well, don't fret. I have something for you. *(Gives him robe)*

Joseph: Oh, Father. It's the most beautiful robe I've ever seen! *(Five brothers enter. Joseph puts coat on)*

Narrator: When the other sons saw the colorful, rich-looking, full-length robe that their father had made for Joseph compared to their own dull, plain, short ones, they knew that their father loved Joseph best. And they were insanely jealous. *(Brothers look at Joseph's coat, at their own, look disgusted)*

Joseph: This little gold wheat pattern reminds me of a dream I had the other night. We were binding sheaves of wheat out in the field, when suddenly my sheaf stood straight up, and all of your sheaves bowed down to mine.

Asher: Perfect. First you strut around in your robe like royalty, now you're actually ruling over us?

Dan: Well, I had a dream, too. In mine, I was a wooden hammer and pounded your wheat to a pulp! *(Hits hand with fist)*

32

Joseph: And in another dream, the sun and moon and eleven stars were bowing down to me.

Reuben: Really, brother. Get a grip. We live in Canaan, not Dreamland.

Narrator: Some time later, Joseph's brothers took the flocks far away to graze, and Jacob asked him to go see how they were doing and report back to him. So Joseph tracked them down.

Gad: Look, brothers, in the distance. Do you see what I see?

Asher: Our little dreamer.

Dan: He is the most annoying kid. Wish I could make him and his dreams go away.

Gad: Well, now's our chance. Father's not here.

Dan: Eee-Gad. I've got a plan. Let's kill him, throw him into an old well, and say that a ferocious animal ate him up.

Narrator: Reuben, the oldest, didn't want to kill his little brother, pesky as he was. So, he planned to come back and rescue him. *(Reuben exits)* When Joseph got there, the brothers stripped him of his robe and threw him into the empty well. Just then, a caravan of Ishmaelites came by on their way to Egypt, their camels loaded with spices and myrrh. *(Ishmaelites enter)*

Dan: Change of plan. Let's sell him to these foreigners, and make a little profit on the side. *(Gives Joseph to Ishmaelite, takes money)*

Narrator: And the evil deed was done. Joseph's brothers sold him for twenty shekels. *(Joseph and Ishmaelites exit)* Some time later, Reuben returned to the well.

Reuben: What have you done? Where's Joseph?

Asher: We sold him. Don't be such a worry-wart. All we have to do is kill a goat, like this ... dip Joseph's robe in the blood, and take it back to Father.

Narrator: So they returned to their father carrying the bloody coat and doing some major overacting.

Dan: *(Sorrowfully)* Father, we found this in the desert. *(All boys look grief-stricken/smirk)*

Jacob: There's no doubt that it's Joseph's. My poor boy — torn to pieces by some ferocious wild animal!

Narrator: Jacob tore his clothes, put on sackcloth, and mourned for many days, refusing to be comforted by his family. *(All exit. Potiphar and Joseph enter)* Meanwhile, the merchants had sold Joseph in Egypt to Potiphar, Pharaoh's captain of the guard.

Potiphar: Joseph, I have noticed what a hard worker you are, and your positive attitude makes you successful at everything you do. I want you to be my personal attendant, in charge of everything that I own.

Narrator: Joseph managed everything so well, that Potiphar had only to worry about his wife, who only had to worry about the handsome Joseph. She got angry when Joseph wouldn't pay any attention to her. So, she got Potiphar to throw him in jail. *(Joseph walks right stage to jail. Enter Cupbearer and Baker)*

Joseph: Why are you two in here?

Cupbearer: We offended Pharaoh.

Baker: And we can't sleep at night because we're having the strangest dreams. If only we knew what they meant.

Joseph: I do dreams. Let me try to help you.

Narrator: Joseph was able to tell the two men what their dreams meant, and the chief cupbearer got out of prison and went back to work for Pharaoh. He forgot all about Joseph until Pharaoh started having strange dreams of his own.

Cupbearer: I know a chap in prison who can tell you what your dream means, sire.

Pharaoh: Bring him to me at once.

Narrator: When Joseph heard Pharaoh's dream about seven fat cows and seven scrawny ones, he explained that God was revealing to Pharaoh that there would be seven years of fabulous crops followed by seven years of famine when nothing would grow.

Pharaoh: You're amazing, Joseph. Even my most trusted magicians could not explain this dream to me. Can you tell me, then, what your God would suggest I do about it?

Joseph: My God would say to find a wise man to put in charge of Egypt, and appoint overseers to take a fifth of each harvest to save for the lean times.

Pharaoh: Since you and your God make such a good team, I want you to be the one in charge of my palace. You will rule over everyone in the palace and the whole land of Egypt except me.

Narrator: So Joseph became the second most powerful man in Egypt, and guided the country through years of plenty and famine. After several years, his starving brothers came to Egypt to get food. *(Five brothers enter and bow center stage)* They bowed down before him, not even recognizing the brother they'd sold as a slave so many years before.

Joseph: Who are you?

Reuben: We are five of twelve brothers, sons of Jacob who lives in Canaan. The youngest is with our father, and one is gone.

Joseph: How do I know that you aren't spies? To make sure that you're telling the truth about this youngest brother, one of you must stay here in prison. The rest can take bags of food home to your families, but you must bring your youngest brother back to me. Then I will release the one in prison, and you will be free to trade here.

Reuben: We will do as you ask. *(Exit around church pews, then return with Benjamin)*

Narrator: So the brothers returned to Egypt the second time with Benjamin. Joseph planted his silver cup in Benjamin's sack and accused him of stealing it, and big brother Reuben offered to stay as a slave if Joseph would let Benjamin return to his father. Finally, Joseph quit playing games.

Joseph: I am Joseph, the one you sold into Egypt.

Dan: Oh, boy. We're goners!

Joseph: Don't be sorry that you sold me here. God sent me ahead of you to save many lives. Go get Father. Tell him that God has made me lord of all Egypt and that I will provide for all of you and your families here. *(Brothers exit around pews, bring back Jacob)*

Narrator: So the brothers brought Jacob and all of their families and flocks to the land of Egypt. Joseph rode out in a splendid chariot to see his father. When he saw Jacob, he threw his arms around him and cried for a very long time. *(Joseph and Jacob hug)*

Jacob: Joseph. You are still alive. Now that I see you with my own eyes, I am ready to die.

Narrator: Pharaoh gave Joseph's family the best land in Egypt, where they all prospered for many years to come — thankful that God's plan is sometimes crazier than our wildest dreams.

Discussion Questions

1. What choice(s) did Joseph make in this skit? What were the consequences?

2. Why were Joseph's brothers so jealous of him? Could he have done anything to lessen their jealousy?

3. What were some of Joseph's talents that helped him get along in life?

4. Why didn't Joseph tell his brothers who he was immediately?

5. Was Joseph bitter that his brothers had sold him into slavery? How can we relate this to our own lives when bad things happen to us?

Related Activities

1. Listen to the CD or watch the video *Joseph and the Amazing Technicolor Dreamcoat,* by Andrew Lloyd Webber. How is it like this skit? How is it different?

2. Look up Genesis 35:23-26 to find out how many mothers Jacob's twelve sons had. Who was Joseph's mother?

3. Read Genesis 29:16-30 to find out how Jacob came to marry Leah and Rachel. Find out who he loved best in Genesis 29:30.

4. Design your own multi-colored robe.

5. Fill in your "Choice Chart" with Character(s), Choice(s), Consequence(s), and Message Learned.

How Low Can You Go?
The Story Of Job

A play based on the book of Job

This skit can be used "bare bones" simply as a reading to spark discussion, or performed as a one-act play using the simplest props.

Scene: The Narrator stands at the lectern or left stage. Job and his Accountant are center stage. The Messengers, Wife, Friends all stand center stage as cued by the Narrator. God and Satan meet right stage or in front of steps if performed in a sanctuary with different levels.

Props: Roll of parchment with numbers written in columns, small table or desk, chair, clipboard, briefcase, bottle of mouthwash, piece of broken pottery, black paper torn up into ashes, cane

Sound Effects: (Optional) Sneaky music played when Satan exits. Cast making sounds like wind blowing, cymbal crashing for thunder during storm

Characters:
If short on actors/actresses, the same person can play Messenger and Friend
Narrator — reader
Accountant — business-like person
Job — righteous man of God
God — the Chief Executive Officer
Angels — optional, non-speaking attendants at staff meeting
Satan — roving staff member
Messenger 1 — Job's servant
Messenger 2 — Job's servant

Messenger 3 — Job's servant
Messenger 4 — Job's servant
Job's Wife — outspoken person
Eliphaz — Job's friend
Bildad — Job's friend
Zophar — Job's friend
Elihus — Job's friend

Time: about 1900 -1800 B.C.

Costumes: Regular street clothes for Narrator; biblical robe for Job, with raggedy-looking burlap wrap for sackcloth to be added, then removed as per script, white beard for ending; white shirt and tie for Accountant; white robe for God; black robe for Satan; white robes, wings, halos for optional Angels; biblical tunics or plain clothes for Servants, Wife, and Friends

---

Narrator: Once in the land of Uz, there lived a man named Job who feared God and stayed away from evil. *(Job stands center stage, hands folded in prayer)*

Accountant: Let's see, Job. *(Unrolls scroll and reads)* Your 1900 B.C. assets include: seven sons, three daughters, 7,000 sheep, 3,000 camels, 500 yoke of oxen, 500 donkeys, and a whole slew of servants.

Narrator: Er, did I mention that he was very rich?

Job: Praise the Lord. I am blessed. I must make an offering for each of my children just in case they have sinned since yesterday morning. *(Kneels in prayer)*

Narrator: In fact, Job was so outstanding, that God couldn't help bragging about him at the angels' monthly staff meeting. *(Action*

40

shifts right stage or in front of stage where God is sitting at a desk with a clipboard in hand, open briefcase on his desk in front of him)

God: Satan, you're here, too? Where have you been?

Satan: Oh, roaming the earth ...

God: Then you must have noticed Job. He doesn't sin, stands up for what's right, and most importantly — respects me.

Satan: Well, why not? You've blocked out anything bad from his life. Take away all he has, and Mr. Perfect Ten will drop to a zero real fast.

God: Prove it. All of his possessions are in your hands, but you may not touch him.

Satan: Yes! Er, I mean, as you wish.

Narrator: Satan wasted no time ruining Job's life. One day, several messengers rushed in on him all at once. *(Satan sneaks off down aisle in audience, rubbing his hands together as he plans his mischief and mayhem. Optional sneaky music. Action shifts back to center stage. Messenger 1 enters)*

Messenger 1: *(Panting, out of breath)* Mr. Job, the Sabeans attacked and took all of your oxen and donkeys. I'm the only one alive to tell the tale.

Messenger 2: Sir, I'm glad I found you. *(Catches breath)* A fire from God burned up all the sheep and servants except me.

Messenger 3: *(Falling to is knees in front of Job)* Master, I have bad news. The Chaldeans have carried off your camels. Luckily I escaped to tell you.

41

Messenger 4: *(Crawls in, speaks from prone position)* My lord, a mighty wind from the desert blew down your oldest son's house, crushing all of your children and servants. No one's alive but me! *(Collapses completely)*

Job: The Lord gave and the Lord has taken away. May his name be praised. *(Messengers exit, shaking their heads in disbelief)*

Narrator: At the next staff meeting in heaven, God talked with Satan again ... *(Scene shifts right stage or in front of steps)*

God: Ah, Satan. Where have you been?

Satan: Roaming the earth.

God: And how did it go with Job? Did any of your nasty tricks work?

Satan: Almost. He's stretched so thin, he's ready to break. Take away his health, and he'll be cursing you by tomorrow night.

God: As you wish. But you may not kill him.

Satan: Right. *(Exits down aisle through audience, cackling evilly. Optional sneaky music)*

Narrator: Again, Satan tried to break Job's spirit, this time with painful sores from head to toe. *(Scene shifts center stage. Job is wearing sackcloth and sitting with his Wife, scratching himself miserably)*

Job's Wife: Ah, Job. Why don't you just hang it up? Curse God and die.

Job: Are you crazy? I took all the good things God gave me in my life; I'll take the bad, too.

Narrator: Job took a piece of pottery and scratched himself as he sat in ashes. A few of his friends came by to try to cheer him up. *(Job scratches himself with pottery. His Wife leaves, and his Friends enter, sitting in a semicircle around him, facing the audience)*

Eliphaz: Hi, Job. Wow. You look bad. Whew! Smell bad, too. You must have really sinned for God to come down on you this hard.

Job: I've done nothing wrong. How dare you blame this on me?

Eliphaz: I'm just saying, maybe you should take your case to God. But before you do, I brought you some mouthwash. *(Hands mouthwash to Job who frowns and pushes it away)*

Bildad: He's right, buddy. Your breath is *ba-a-d*! And you're going to have to confess your sins if you want to stop suffering ...

Job: Confess what? I haven't done anything wrong!

Zophar: It could be even worse for a *major* sinner like you. At least you've still got your wife and good friends like us here to cheer you up.

Elihu: Maybe God's just bringing all this trouble on to make you a better person, like boot camp in the Marines. My advice? Keep quiet, and hang in there.

Job: A-a-a-a-rgh! God, just tell me *why* I'm suffering?

Narrator: *(Lights switch on and off. Optional sound effects: cast makes blowing noises like the wind, cymbal crash for thunder)* The Lord answered Job out of a storm:

God: *(Standing on his desk right stage, speaking with booming voice)* Who are you to question me? Can you answer MY questions? Where were you when the earth was created? Who makes the eagle soar or watches over baby animals being born in the wild? And one more thing — why do you listen to your clueless friends?

Job: You're right, God. I'm in way over my head. I don't understand your ways, and shouldn't be asking you why. I'll just work with what I have ... Please forgive me.

Narrator: And God did. In fact, over time he blessed him twice as much as he had before. *(Friends exit. Job stands up, turns back to audience, removes sackcloth, and puts on fake white beard, leaning forward on cane. Turns around to face audience as Accountant enters with scroll)*

Accountant: Whew, Job! You're 140 years old, and just look at your assets. You have seven sons, three beautiful daughters who will split their inheritance with the boys (unheard of!), 14,000 sheep, 6,000 camels, 1,000 yoke of oxen, and 1,000 donkeys.

Job: *(Looking up to heaven with hands clasped in prayer)* Thank you, God.

Narrator: And no thanks to Satan, who by the way, stopped showing up at staff meetings in heaven. They say he's looking for a new *Job*.

Discussion Questions
1. What choices did Job make in this skit?

2. Have you ever had a low point when you thought things couldn't get any worse — and they did? What did you do?

3. Who do you listen to when you're low — your family, your friends, God? Which is the most reliable?

4. What do you do if God doesn't seem to be answering your prayers right away?

5. Why do you think it was unusual for a girl to get an inheritance along with her brothers?

Related Activities
1. Make props for the play:
    a. A scroll can be made using a long piece of paper, gluing a stick or dowel rod at each end so it can be rolled, and tying it with a leather shoestring or piece of yarn or ribbon. Two columns can be included: 1900 B.C. assets and 1800 B.C. assets. Figures can be taken from skit or researched in Job 1:2 and Job 42:12.
    b. Sackcloth can be made by cutting a neck and arm holes in a burlap bag. Cutting or tearing black or gray paper into small pieces will make the ashes.
    c. God's briefcase and clipboard could be labeled with a title or bumper sticker that the students make up, e.g., God: C.E.O. (Combating Evil Ones); God; M.P. (Master Planner); or Suffering Happens.

2. Have each student write something that is worrying him/her on a piece of paper (signed or unsigned). Collect them and keep them in a basket or jar for the rest of the year. Pray each week that God will help with these concerns. At the end of the year, reread the worries and see how God has worked over time.

3. Read what Jesus says about worrying in Matthew 6:25-34. Make a list of reasons not to worry. Decorate with birds, lilies, and grass as per the scripture.

4. Add the Job story to your master chart: Character(s), Choice(s) Made, Consequence(s), and Message Learned from his Life.

Moses Rocks!

A play based on the books
of Exodus and Numbers

This play is designed to be performed as "Reader's Theater" with no props or scenery, or as a simple one-act skit with minimal effects. It would best be showcased in a sanctuary or stage area with two levels joined by stairs.

Scenes: Narrator at lectern, left stage; river is in front of center stage steps; well is right stage; Jethro's home is right stage in front of steps; burning bush is center stage. Pharaoh is on stage as scene opens.

Props: Doll, basket to hold baby, bucket, optional sheep stuffed animals, bush, red crepe paper streamers. Optional scenery: blue sheet held and waved by two non-speakers in front of center stage steps for river; backdrop of Mount Sinai center stage; scene showing well right stage

Characters:
Narrator — reader
Pharaoh — leader of the Egyptians
Mom — Moses' Hebrew mother
Sister — Moses' Hebrew sister
Pharaoh's Daughter — adopted Moses and gave him Egyptian education
Servant — to Pharaoh's daughter
Slave Master — Egyptian who beats Hebrew Slave / non-speaking
Slave — Hebrew beaten by Egyptian / non-speaking
Jethro — Midian priest and father of Zipporah

Shepherd 1 — bully at the well, non-speaking (can be same as Slave Master)

Shepherd 2 — bully at well, non-speaking (can be same as Hebrew slave)

Zipporah — Jethro's daughter who marries Moses

Time: about 1526-1410 B.C.

Costumes: Biblical robes and scarves for Mom, Sister, Hebrew Slave, Jethro, and Zipporah; biblical robe, sash, sandals, and staff for Moses; Egyptian robes (purple or gold cloth) for Pharaoh, Pharaoh's Daughter, Servant, and Slave Master, with royalty wearing crowns

---

Narrator: This is the story of a Jewish boy named Moses who grew up to lead his people out of Egypt. If you'll recall, Joseph (of coat-of-many-colors-fame) and his Hebrew family had settled in the land of Goshen in Egypt, where Joseph served for many years as Pharaoh's number two man. The Jews had been fruitful and multiplied, and many years had passed so that the new Egyptian kings didn't even remember who Joseph was.

Pharaoh: What is it with those Jews? They keep multiplying — and I don't mean doing math problems. Just think what would happen if they decided to go to war against us. We must put them to work as slaves, so they have no time to think of rebellion.

Narrator: So the Hebrews became slaves to Egyptian bosses who worked them cruelly, making bricks, mixing mortar, building cities, and working in the fields. Though the lives of the Hebrews were miserable, still their numbers grew by leaps and bounds.

Pharaoh: That's it. Time to take strong action. I decree that every boy that is born to a Jew must be thrown into the Nile, but let every girl live.

Narrator: Whoa! This was one of the few times in the Bible when it was good to be a girl! Anyway, at about this same time, a young Jewish couple had a fine baby boy.

Mom: *(Enters with Baby and Sister and stands in front of steps, center stage)* It's not *fair-oh*, Pharaoh. I've hidden this baby for three months, but with his lusty cry, the Egyptians are bound to find him soon.

Sister: Pharaoh said the boys must be thrown in the Nile, right?

Mom: Yes, but I can't bear to do it.

Sister: Sure you can — in his own personal boat, of course.

Mom: You're a genius. Bring me a papyrus basket and some tar and pitch. A little water-proofing, and his little boat is ready. Lay him in gently, and take him among the reeds along the bank of the Nile. Then stay and watch at a distance. *(Mom exits. Sister places basket on top step and kneels down right stage pretending to hide behind reeds)*

Narrator: The faithful sister did as she was told. The little basket rocked gently, and the baby cooed and snoozed. Soon, Pharaoh's daughter came down to the river to bathe. *(Pharaoh's Daughter and her Servant enter center stage)*

Pharaoh's Daughter: A tisket, a tasket. I see a floating basket! Servant, go fetch it from the reeds for me.

Servant: *(Pretends to wade into water, returns with basket)* Yes, my lady. Look what's inside.

Pharaoh's Daughter: All I can say is — that baby *rocks*!

Servant: I dare say, you would, too, if you were floating in a boat on the river. He must be one of the Hebrew babies. One thing for sure, he has good lungs.

Pharaoh's Daughter: Poor thing. He's probably starving. Got milk?

Sister: *(Coming out from hiding to stand center stage)* Excuse me, I could go and get one of the Hebrew women to nurse that baby for you.

Pharaoh's Daughter: Great idea.

Narrator: So the girl ran and got the baby's mother. *(Sister exits and returns with Mom)*

Pharaoh's Daughter: I'll pay you to take this baby and nurse him for me. *(Mom smiles happily and takes baby in arms)*

Narrator: Such a deal. Not only did the baby get his real mother's milk and a healthy dose of training in Hebrew religion and history, but he was later adopted by Pharaoh's daughter who named him Moses and gave him a proper Egyptian education. *(Mom, Sister, Pharaoh's Daughter, Servant exit. Older Moses enters)* Now, if Moses couldn't find trouble, then trouble would find Moses. One day, as he was watching his own people working their fingers to the bone, an Egyptian began beating one of the Hebrew slaves.

Moses: Hey, man. What are you doing? Stop that now. *(Hits fist into hand, then runs down center aisle, walking back up side aisle to sit right stage)*

Narrator: He killed the Egyptian and buried him in the sand. Pharaoh was not pleased when he found out, and tried to kill Moses, who fled to a place called Midian. Moses was just minding his own business, sitting by a well when seven girls came to draw water for the flocks of their father. *(Zipporah enters with bucket and pretends to fill it)* Some bullying shepherds came along and tried to drive them away, so what could Moses do? *(Shepherds enter, block well, pull off her scarf)*

50

Moses: What are you doing? Stop that now. *(Pushes Shepherds away from well)*

Narrator: Remember, Moses was a highly-trained Egyptian prince, a fact which the *sheps* had not *herd*. They were no match for him, and Moses saved the fair maidens. *(Shepherds exit to center stage where they hide behind bush. Zipporah walks down steps to right stage)* The girls hoofed it home to report to dad, a Midian priest named Jethro.

Jethro: Why are you girls home so early?

Zipporah: An Egyptian rescued us from some shepherds and even watered the flocks for us.

Narrator: So, Moses was invited to supper, and ended up marrying Zipporah and tending sheep for Jethro, his father-in-law. While on the far side of the desert, Moses came to the mountain of God, where an angel of the Lord appeared to him in flames of fire from within a bush. *(Moses walks center stage and sees burning bush, which has non-speakers behind it waving red crepe paper strips)*

Moses: That's a hunk-of, hunk-of burning bush! Why doesn't the bush burn up?

Narrator: When he got closer, God called to him from within the bush.

God: Moses! Moses!

Moses: Here I am!

God: I am the God of Abraham, Isaac, and Jacob. I have seen how miserable my people are in Egypt, and I want you to free them. *(Moses kneels in front of bush)*

Narrator: Isn't it awesome the way that God perfectly molded Moses for the job of negotiating for the freedom of the Jews with the Egyptian Pharaoh? Anyway, Moses had his work cut out for him in freeing the Jews. With the help of God, and snakes, frogs, bloody water, gnats, flies, livestock diseases, boils, hail, locusts, darkness, and finally death to the firstborn Egyptians, Moses got Pharaoh's attention, and the Jews left Egypt. *(Moses stands firmly center stage with staff in front of him ready to defend himself)*

Moses: Time to make our exit-odus. *(Moses taps staff on ground as if talking to group of people)*

Narrator: *(To Moses)* That's Exodus. A whole book in the Bible tells how God parts the Red Sea so that you can lead the Hebrews through it, then the water rushes back drowning all of the Egyptians who try to follow you.

Moses: *(To Narrator)* You don't say. Does it tell what happened next?

Narrator: Well, the book of Numbers tells how you strike a rock with your staff at Mount Sinai in the desert and water pours out of it for your thirsty people to drink. Then, the book of Exodus tells how God gave you the Ten Commandments and instructions for building a tabernacle to worship him.

Moses: Yes, and God's little stone instruction booklet helped us learn how important it is to obey the Lord and it gave us standards to live by. Too bad my people were such complainers, and even I disobeyed once. None of my generation entered Canaan, but Joshua fought for seven years so that Israel could gain control of the Promised Land, and the job I started could be finished.

Narrator: Well, in looking back over your life, Moses. It's clear that you led the Hebrew people through some pretty *rocky* times. First you, *rocked* in your little papyrus boat, then you struck a *rock* which gushed water for the people to drink, and finally you brought down sacred *rocks* with God's Ten Commandments for the people. All we can say is, thanks for your leadership, and *rock* on, Brother Moses! *(Moses nods and smiles happily. Whole cast enters, and follows Moses down center aisle, moving to the tune of a Christian rock song)*

Discussion Questions

1. Why was Moses the perfect person to lead the Hebrews out of Egypt?

2. What choice did Moses make when he saw the Egyptian master beating a Hebrew slave? What was the consequence of this choice? What choice did Moses make when the shepherds were bullying the girls at the well? What were the consequences of this choice?

3. Read Exodus 12:5-7 and Exodus 12:14-16 to find out about the Passover. Discuss what you would think today if someone told you God wanted you to mark your door to show you were a Christian.

4. Read Numbers 20:8-12. The Lord is angry that Moses didn't speak to the rock as instructed, then took credit for the miracle of the water gushing from the rock. Was the Lord's punishment too harsh?

5. Tell three ways that Moses helped the Hebrews.

Related Activities

1. Read Exodus 2:3 to find out how Moses' mom made the waterproof basket. Brainstorm ways you could make a waterproof basket today. Try out your hypotheses.

2. Make scenery for the play. Paint a backdrop on a large piece of cardboard for Mount Sinai and the well at Midian. Paint and cut out a bush to set in front of the mountain.

3. Read Exodus 12:5-7 and Exodus 12:12-13 to find out what the Passover is. How did God know which houses to pass over?

4. Assign a different student to read each passage and tell the group what excuses Moses tried to give God for not choosing him to lead the Hebrews and God's answers to him: Exodus 3:13-14, Exodus 4:1-3, Exodus 4:10-12, and Exodus 4:13-15. Write their answers on a chart or chalkboard in two columns: Moses' excuse, God's answer.

5. Read Hebrews 11:24-30 to find examples of Moses' faith in God. Have a student draw a poster to illustrate each.

6. Add Moses' name to your Chart of Bible Character(s), Choice(s), Consequence(s), and Message Learned. (Deuteronomy 34:10-12 gives a good summary of why Moses is remembered.)

Glean On Me:
The Story Of Ruth

A play based on the book of Ruth

This play is meant to be performed as simply as possible in one continuous act. It can be read as a "Reader's Theater" piece, or performed with minimal props and scenery, preferably in a sanctuary or stage with two levels.

Scenes: Stage left in front of stage steps is Moab with an easel holding a sleazy sign; center stage is Judah, with a basket of wheat sitting in Boaz's field; in front of center stage steps is Naomi's house in Judah; right stage is the threshing room floor with tent. Narrator stands at lectern with microphone.

Props: Easel with Moab sign, optional baskets or suitcases for Naomi and Ruth, basket of wheat, sticks for men to pound wheat, tent for threshing room floor, blankets to use as bedrolls

Characters:
Narrator — reader
Elimelech — Naomi's husband that dies in Judah
Naomi — Ruth and Orpah's mother-in-law
Mahlon — non-seaking
Kilion — non-speaking
Ruth — woman from Moab who moves to Judah with Naomi
Orpah — woman from Moab who stays there
Townsperson — resident of Judah
Boaz — relative of Naomi's husband who owns fields in Judah
Harvester — worker in Boaz's fields
Kinsman-Redeemer — closer relative to Naomi than Boaz

Time: written sometime between 1375-1050 B.C.

55

Costumes: Biblical robes, scarves, and sandals for all characters except Narrator, who dresses in today's style

---

Narrator: When food became very scarce in Bethlehem in Judah, a man named Elimelech moved his wife, Naomi, and two sons to Moab. This was a bold step, as the Jews hated the Moabites so much that it was against Jewish law to marry a Moabite.

Elimelech: *(Standing center stage in Judah with Naomi, Mahlon, and Kilion)* Naomi, we must move our sons, Mahlon and Kilion, outside the Promised Land to Moab, or we'll all starve.

Naomi: Must we go to that sleezy, sinful town? It's full of — Moabites — who wouldn't even let the Jews pass through their lands during our escape from Egypt. Just promise me we'll return to Judah as soon as possible.

Elimelech: Cross my heart and hope to die. *(Family walks down steps to left stage, Moab)*

Narrator: That "hope to die" part proved to be a poor choice of words, for after about ten years, Elimelech died in Moab. *(Elimelech exits)* He left behind his widow, Naomi, and their two sons, who married Moabite women named Orpah and Ruth. *(Orpah and Ruth enter)*

Ruth: Thank you for accepting us as your daughters, Naomi. I know most Jewish women would rather die than have their sons marry Moabites.

Naomi: You have seen and heard much about my God in all the years that we have known each other, and have probably come to know him nearly as well as I. It is not up to me to judge you.

Narrator: Though Naomi made the best of her husband's death, more sorrow soon came her way. Both of her sons died, and she was left alone. She heard that there was food again in Judah so she decided to go back home with her two daughters-in-law. On the road back to Bethlehem, Naomi had a change of heart. *(Naomi, Ruth, Orpah walk in front of center stage steps with suitcases/baskets)*

Naomi: Stop! You girls should go back to your own mothers. Maybe then you could find new husbands.

Narrator: She kissed both girls and they had a big sob fest.

Orpah: No, we'll go back to Judah with you.

Narrator: More tears.

Naomi: Why would you want to come to a land of strangers? I'm too old to have any more sons, and the Jewish men would stick up their noses at Moabite women — and widows to boot. No, you must go home, so you don't become an old maid like me. Oh, how the Lord has turned against me!

Narrator: Tear ducts now working serious overtime ...

Orpah: You're right, Naomi. Moab's the safer choice. Have a nice life, you two. Kiss, kiss. I'm out of here! *(Orpah exits)*

Naomi: Ruth, your sister in-law is going back to her own people and gods. Go with her.

Ruth: Don't tell me to turn my back on you. Wherever you go, I'm going. Your people and your God will be mine. End of story.

Naomi: Is that your final answer?

Ruth: Yes. Let's get going.

Narrator: So the two women went to Bethlehem, where they caused quite a stir. *(Naomi and Ruth walk up stairs to Judah, center stage. Townsperson enters with basket of wheat)*

Townsperson: Can this be the same Naomi who left us so many years ago?

Naomi: Don't call me Naomi any more. The old Naomi had a husband, two sons, and a life. That Naomi's gone. *(Dramatically)* Call me Mara, because my life has become bitter. The Lord has brought me great troubles.

Townsperson: Why don't you tell us how you really feel, Naomi?

Narrator: Anyway, the two got to Bethlehem just as the spring barley harvest was beginning. Since Naomi's husband had a relative named Boaz in the area, Ruth went to his fields to glean. (Gleaning was a Jewish custom in which land owners left some of the grain in the fields behind for poor people and widows to pick up.) *(Townsperson gives Ruth her basket and exits. Ruth stoops and pretends to pick up wheat and put in her basket. Harvester enters, supervising workers)*

Boaz: *(Enters)* Greetings, harvesters. The Lord be with you.

Harvester: And also with you!

Boaz: Foreman, who is that young woman?

Harvester: She came back from Moab with Naomi. Nice person — and a hard worker. She asked if she could glean after us, and has been working since morning.

Narrator: Boaz went to Ruth.

Boaz: Daughter, stay here with my servant girls and glean only in this field where you'll be safe. Help yourself to the water from those jars over there, and feel free to "glean on me" anytime you like.

Ruth: Thank you. But why are you being so kind to a foreigner?

Boaz: I heard about all the things you've done for your mother-in-law, and how you left your own people and came to a strange land. May God reward your kindness.

Narrator: At dinner, Boaz let her dip her bread in the wine with the other harvesters, and gave her roasted grain (half of which she pocketed to take home to Naomi). After she went back to work, he told his men to leave extra stalks for her to pick up, so she returned home with quite an armload. *(Boaz, Harvester exit to threshing floor, stage right and pretend to thresh/pound wheat, then freeze. Naomi enters and stands in front of steps center stage. Ruth walks down steps to greet her)*

Naomi: Wow, you're loaded. Where did you get all that? Tell me about your day.

Ruth: I worked in the field of a man named Boaz who said that I could glean on him.

Naomi: Bless him! Wait, did you say *Boaz*? He's our relative. That means he's our kinsman-redeemer. That means that, according to Jewish custom, he could volunteer to take care of his extended family, being us. That means he could *marry* the widow of his relative.

Narrator: So Ruth worked with the girls in Boaz's field until the fall wheat harvest was over and lived with Naomi, who had thought of a plan.

Naomi: Ruth, tonight Boaz will stay by the threshing room floor where the wheat is crushed, to protect his crop. Get yourself cleaned up, put on some perfume and your best robe. Then, creep up to his bedroll after dinner, uncover his feet and lay down, but don't let anyone see you. He'll tell you what to do next.

Narrator: This may sound like a strange plan, but in Jewish tradition, the servant often slept at the master's feet, sometimes even sharing his blanket. This would signal Boaz that he could be her kinsman-redeemer. So Ruth did as her mother-in-law advised — no questions asked. *(Naomi freezes. Boaz and Harvester lay down; Ruth walks right stage and curls up at Boaz's feet)*

Boaz: Who are you?

Ruth: Your servant, Ruth. Please share some of your cover with me because you're my kinsman-redeemer.

Boaz: God bless you, daughter. You're a noble person, as everyone in Judah knows. I'll be happy to help you, but there's one man that is a closer relative than I. He has first dibs on taking care of you. I'll talk to him in the morning. Meanwhile, just take this barley home to Naomi and sneak away so no one sees that you were on the threshing room floor.

Narrator: *(Ruth walks down steps in front of center stage)* Naomi, of course, wanted all the details.

Naomi: Oh, Ruth. I have a *good* feeling about this man. He won't rest until he settles this matter today.

Narrator: And Boaz did settle it. The closer kin gave Boaz the right to care for Naomi and Ruth, and Boaz married her. They loved and respected each other, and of course, took good care of Naomi in her old age.

Naomi: I knew that everything would turn out just fine for you in Bethlehem.

Ruth: The perfect place for our new baby to be born.

Naomi: What? You're having a baby? Thank you, Lord. This is a job for Nana Naomi. Of course it'll be a boy. I'll care for him and raise him up properly in the eyes of the Lord.

Ruth: First Naomi, then, Mara, "the bitter one," now Nana. You sure change names a lot.

Narrator: Hug and kiss. Ruth and Boaz did have a child, named Obed. As it turns out, he wasn't the only outstanding baby in the family to be born in Bethlehem. His grandson would be David, a direct ancestor of Jesus. Those Moab genes sure made for one perfect Savior!

Discussion Questions

1. What choices did Ruth make in this story? What were the consequences?

2. How do you think Boaz's neighbors might react to him marrying a Moabitess (woman from Moab)?

3. Why do you think God might choose a Moabitess to be one of Jesus' ancestors?

4. How did Naomi and Ruth help each other?

5. Do you think it pleases God when young people listen to older ones?

Related Activities

1. Make props/scenery for the play:
   a. A flashy sign for Moab that shows that it is a sinful place (The Slee-Zee Saloon, Open 24 hours, Free Drinks, Dog Fights, Girls, girls, girls ...)
   b. Make a tent from a blanket thrown over some type of frame — some easels, coat racks, or upended tables.

2. Read how the transfer of property became final in Ruth 4:7-8. Draw a cartoon of two people today making a deal at the bank, car lot, store, White House, or school using this biblical method.

3. Read Genesis 19:30-37 to find out who the Moabs were descended from. Read 2 Kings 3:21-27 to find out why the Moabs may have hated the Jews.

4. Look up this key verse in Ruth 1:16. Make a class mural showing the main scenes from Ruth's story, using words from this verse as a title.

5. Add Naomi, Ruth, and Boaz to your master chart of Character(s), Choice(s), Consequence(s), and Message Learned.

Solomon The Wise: You Be The Judge

A play based on 1 Kings 3, 2 Chronicles 1, and Ecclesiastes 3

This play is designed to be read and discussed with no properties, or presented in one act with minimum scenery and props. The action occurs in one continuous act with no scene changes. A sanctuary or auditorium with steps would be ideal for its presentation.

Scenes: The dream scene takes place off center stage at a different level, such as at the bottom of the stairs, or in front of the lectern; the rest of the play takes place center stage in the royal palace in Jerusalem with two servants stationed on either side of throne. Narrator stands at lectern or off to the side. God may stand at different lectern or on a higher level. Servants stand center stage on either side of the throne throughout the entire play, slowly fanning Solomon. (Optional action: popping grapes into Solomon's mouth.)

Props: In front of stage area: table and chair, royal pillow. Center stage: throne or royal settee (use minister's chair or bench), palm branches, optional grapes, fake sword, baby doll, clipboard for Aide, accountant's scroll with numbers written on it, briefcase

Characters:
Narrator — reader
God — the Almighty
Solomon — a wise king
Servant(s) — one or two non-speakers
King's Aide — efficient, organized
Woman 1 — recent mother

63

Woman 2 — recent mother
Accountant — conservative executive

Time: about 970 B.C.

Costumes: Regular clothes for Narrator; white robe for God; king's robe/crown for Solomon; biblical dress for Servant and two Women; biblical robe with necktie and briefcase for Accountant

---

Narrator: There was once a young man named Solomon who became king of the Israelites after the death of his great father, David. Soon after taking the job, the Lord appeared to Solomon in a dream.

God: Ask for anything you want.

Solomon: *(Sitting at table with head down on pillow, snoring. Head jerks up and eyes open when God speaks)* Let me see ... I'm just a kid who is supposed to rule over an entire kingdom. What I'd *really* like is the wisdom to choose between right and wrong so I can be a good leader.

God: *(Standing above Solomon)* I'm impressed that you didn't ask for long life, wealth, or to have all of your enemies rubbed out. I'll give you a wise heart, and also wealth and honor so that you will be the greatest king of your time.

Solomon: Wow. Thank you. *(Snores on for a moment, then stretches and yawns)* Just think of being the wisest man in the whole world ... *(Gets up from table and walks center stage to palace in Jerusalem)*

Narrator: Solomon went back to Jerusalem where he soon began to realize that God really had granted him special wisdom, as on the day when two women came to see him. *(Two Women and King's*

Aide carrying a baby, sword, and clipboard enter and stand before throne)

Woman 1: My lord, we both live in the same house and have given birth to babies within the last three days. No one else was around to be a witness, but her baby died during the night so she got up while I was sleeping and switched babies. When I woke up, the dead baby was sleeping by me, and my baby was with her.

Woman 2: Liar. The living one is *my* son. The dead one is yours.

Woman 1: I saw in the morning light that the dead baby was not mine. Mine is alive.

Woman 2: It's mine. *(Grabs baby from Aide)*

Woman 1: No, it's mine. *(Grabs baby from Woman 2)*

Woman 2: Mine. *(Tugs baby's arm)*

Woman 1: Mine. *(Pulling baby's other arm. Neither lets go — fighting over baby)*

Solomon: Whoa! Ladies. Let me get this straight. You say your son is alive and hers is dead, and you say that *your* son is alive and *hers* is dead. I know just how to solve this disagreement fairly. Bring me my sword.

King's Aide: *(Pulls out sword)* Here, sire. Freshly sharpened. *(Touches point with finger)*

Solomon: Excellent. Now, cut the living child in two. Give half to her, and half to her.

Woman 2: Great idea!

Woman 1: *No!* Please, my lord, give her the baby. *(Hands baby to Woman 2. Sinks to her knees, begging King Solomon)* Don't kill him!

Solomon: Servant, don't kill that baby. I've made my decision. I know who the mother is.

Narrator: Now, *you be the judge* ... Who was the real mother, and how did Solomon know this? *(Stop skit while audience answers questions. Aide gives baby to Woman 1. Both Women exit)*

Narrator: Wow — you're very wise, too. From that point on, everyone was pretty much in awe of Solomon because they saw that he had the wisdom from God to make fair decisions. Solomon was wise in many other ways, too.

King's Aide: *(Looking at clipboard)* King Solomon, I have this week's lecture schedule for you. Monday you'll present some of your 3,000 proverbs and 5,005 songs at the synagogue. Tuesday you'll discuss local plant and animal life for the Boy Scouts; Saturday you will meet with a group of kings who admire your wisdom, and Sunday, of course, is your day of rest.

Solomon: Very good. Oh, and send me the royal accountant, please. I need an update of my financial status. *(King's Aide exits. Accountant enters with scroll)*

Accountant: *(Unrolling scroll to read)* As of 10:30 this morning, you have 1,400 chariots and 12,000 horses, sire, with 24 expecting foals any day now.

Solomon: Ah, it is their time to be born. There is a time for everything, and a season for every activity under heaven: a time to be born and a time to die, a time to tear down and a time to build. Hey, I like that. Think I'll write up a song about that. Speaking of building, what's the status on the Temple?

Accountant: On schedule, sire. 30,000 men from Israel have been sent off to Lebanon for cedar, 70,000 are carriers, 80,000 are stone-cutters, and 3,300 are supervisors. The contractor says it'll take about seven years to complete the whole project. *(Accountant exits)*

Narrator: So, it would seem that Solomon had it all. *(Servant pops grape into Solomon's mouth)* He was wise, rich beyond belief, and obeyed God. Actually, there was one tiny rule that he ignored. God didn't want the Israelites to marry foreign women, because they would worship their wives' gods instead of him. Solomon, however, married often and well, and was soon getting ready for another wedding to a Moabitess.

Solomon: *(Whispering to Aide)* A Moabitess?

King's Aide: A lady from Moab, sire.

Solomon: Oh, right. Is my tux ready?

King's Aide: Sorry, your majesty. There hasn't been time to get it cleaned since your last wedding.

Solomon: Never mind, her daddy's a tailor. I'll have him make me a new one. *(Whispers to Aide)* One of the perks of having a rich wife, you know ...

King's Aide: If you'll pardon my curiosity, how many wives does that make for you, sire?

Solomon: She will be number 700, not including my 300 concubines.

Narrator: Concubines were women that King Solomon didn't marry, but just kept on the side. Now, *you be the judge* ... Was it a good idea to have seven hundred wives? Why or why not? *(Narrator pauses to give audience time to answer)*

Narrator: At any rate, Solomon's heart did, indeed, turn away from God. He even built a high place for the detestable god of Moab and offered sacrifices to him.

God: *(Standing above Solomon from lectern or chair)* Solomon, I've warned you twice to keep my commandments, but you haven't listened. Since you continue to disobey, I will tear your kingdom away. For the sake of your father, David, I will take it from your son, not you. *(Solomon hangs his head sadly)*

Narrator: After he reigned over Jerusalem forty years, Solomon died. *(Solomon lies down on floor as if dead. Servants place grapes on his chest like flowers and fan him)* His son's kingdom was divided, as God had promised. But his wisdom lives on in the books of Proverbs, Ecclesiastes, and Song of Songs in the Bible. Was Solomon's wisdom enough to make him a happy man? *You be the judge ...*

Discussion Questions
1. Did wisdom make Solomon a happy man?

2. Why didn't God want Solomon to marry outside his faith?

3. What poor choice(s) did Solomon make?

4. What were the consequences of his choice(s)?

5. Do you think God's consequences were fair? Why/why not?

Related Activities
1. Make a chart with the headings: Building Materials, Carvings, Furniture. Assign different students to skim 1 Kings 6:20-22, 1 Kings 7:27-29, 1 Kings 7:36, and 1 Kings 7:58-50 to find examples of building materials, carvings, and furniture found in the Temple Solomon built for God, and fill them in on your

chart. Have another student check 1 Kings 6:37 to find out how long it took to build the Temple.

2. Solomon also built himself a grand palace described in 1 Kings 7:1-12. Design your own dream palace, making sure to use building materials, and carving designs found in your own area. Assign a student to check in 1 Kings 7:1 to find out how long it took to build Solomon's palace.

3. Read Ecclesiastes 3, "A Time for Everything." Let each student choose a line to illustrate and make a book, or play a guessing game in which students act out a line, and the group guesses which line he/she is acting out.

4. Read some of Solomon's advice, Proverbs 19-22. Have each student choose his/her favorite wise saying to illustrate or make up one of his/her own. Write them on scrolls and share them with the younger children.

5. Fill in chart with Character(s), Choice(s), Consequence(s), and Message Learned.

Courageous Cousins:
Esther And Mordecai

A play based on the book of Esther

This play can simply be read without stage directions to promote discussion of a great Bible story, or it can be presented with some simple scenery and props. The best setting would be a sanctuary or auditorium with steps up to the main staging area.

Scenes: Though this is technically a one-act play, the scenes change continuously to different areas of the stage. Two thrones sit in the royal palace, center stage, while the palace gate is at a lower level in front of the steps. Right stage is the royal sitting room with a bench and fancy pillow. Lower left stage is the home of Mordecai and Esther. Narrator stands at lectern.

Props: Center stage: two thrones (chairs with fancy pillows) with royal scepter leaning against one, book of annals and quill pen on small table beside other one, goblets. In front of steps: stool for Mordecai; right stage (sitting room) bench with fancy pillow or settee, poster board, magic marker. Left stage (behind lectern) banquet table set with dishes/utensils, two extra chairs

Characters:
Narrator — reader
Zethar — king's eunuch and advisor
King Xerxes — ruler of Persia
Queen Vashti — wife of King Xerxes before Esther
Military Leader — guest at the king's palace
Prince — guest at the banquet
Esther — Jewish girl who becomes queen
Mordecai — Esther's cousin who works at the palace gate

71

Hathach — royal messenger / non-speaking part
Haman — evil advisor

Time: about 486-473 B.C.

Costumes: Regular modern clothes for narrator; biblical robes for Zethar, Mordecai, Hathach, and Haman. Add royal robes and crowns for king, queens, and prince. Add swords or breast-plates for military leader and prince.

Narrator: *(King Xerxes is sitting in his throne center stage with Zethar at his side)* This is the story of how a faithful girl named Esther and her cousin, Mordecai, saved the Jewish people. Esther was an orphan who was raised by Mordecai in the town of Susa where King Xerxes of Persia also lived. One day the king called for his trusted *eunuch.*

King: Zethar, which goblets shall we use for our fabulous seven-day banquet? I want to impress all the military leaders before we attack Greece.

Zethar: The gold ones, sire. And each guest should have a different goblet and drink as much wine as he likes.

King: Right. Now, on to the important details. Shall I have the royal hair stylist weave emeralds into my beard or rubies?

Zethar: Why not have both?

King: Smashing idea. After all, I *am* the king!

Narrator: Soon, the military leaders and princes arrived for the banquet and were shown into the royal palace. *(Zethar enters leading Military Leaders and Prince, who stand center stage next to King drinking wine from goblets)*

King: *(In high spirits from the wine)* Enough talk of war. Zethar, I think it's time to show my good friends my beautiful wife, Queen Vashti. *(Men all nod and raise goblets in air)*

Zethar: *(Zethar enters sitting chamber, stage right. Queen is sitting on bench brushing her hair)* I have a message from the King. He asks that you join him at the banquet.

Queen: That drunken fool. He knows that it is against Persian custom for a woman to display herself at a public gathering of men. Tell him the *Queen* will not be *seen. (Zethar reports back to King center stage. Queen strides off down side aisle)*

Military Leader: A king who would attack mighty Greece cannot control his own wife?

Prince: A woman should know her place!

Narrator: Burning with anger, the king called his law experts to ask their advice. Afraid that the Queen's refusal would trickle down to all women who would then disrespect their husbands, they took a firm stand.

King: *(To his Military Leaders)* Women must know their places. Therefore, I decree that every man shall be ruler over his own household. As for Queen Vashti, she will never be allowed in my presence again. Nah, nah, nah, nah-nah! *(Sticks out tongue and wiggles fingers from his ears in direction of Queen. King and Zethar freeze center stage)*

Narrator: After the king's anger died down, he was lonely. His advisors suggested he bring beautiful girls from all parts of the kingdom into his *harem.* Then he could choose his favorite to become his new wife. So messengers were sent to all parts of the kingdom to bring back the women. A few days later, Esther told Mordecai that she'd been chosen to go live at the palace.

73

Mordecai: *(Esther and Mordecai stand in front of steps, stage left)* I'm not surprised, for you are truly a great beauty. Go with my blessings, but don't tell anyone you're a Jew or that we're related. We'll keep in touch through messengers. *(Mordecai exits. Esther climbs steps to royal sitting room and sits down on the bench)*

King: Zethar, having all these beautiful girls come to the palace to receive special diets and beauty treatments for a year was a stroke of genius. *(Peeks into royal chamber and sees Esther rubbing lotion on her arm)* That one has really found favor in my eyes. Should I choose her to be my new wife?

Zethar: She's lovely, sire. And more importantly, she seems smart and kind.

Narrator: So King Xerxes chose Esther to be his wife and they were soon married. *(Esther puts on crown and joins King center stage, sitting in throne next to him. Zethar and Hathach stand on either side. Mordecai enters and sits below steps center stage at the gate)* Meanwhile, Mordecai, who sat at the king's gate, overheard two nobles plotting to kill the king. He reported this to Esther who warned the king.

King: Thank you, Queen Esther. I might be dead now if it weren't for you.

Esther: It was not I who saved your life, majesty, but Mordecai. Let his name be written in the book of *annals*. *(She nods to Zethar who writes in the book. Everyone on stage freezes)*

Narrator: Sometime later, a proud man named Haman became the king's most honored advisor. *(Haman enters, passing Mordecai who does not bow)*

Haman: *(To himself)* So, the Jew doesn't bow to his superiors? We'll see about that! *(Marches up stairs to stand by King, bumping Esther out of the way)* King, I'd like a word, please. ALONE!

(Esther and Hathach exit to sitting room; Zethar backs up away from throne. Haman whispers to King, who nods)

Narrator: Haman talked the king into making a decree. All Jews would be killed on the thirteenth day of the month of Adar. When Mordecai found out about the law, he sent a messenger to Esther telling her to plead with the king for their people. *(King, Haman, and Zethar freeze in position)*

Esther: Hathach, tell Mordecai I cannot just talk to the king any time I want. By law, anyone who approaches the king in the inner court without being summoned will be put to death unless the king offers a gold *scepter* to spare his/her life. Remember what happened to his last wife? *(Hathach walks down steps to Mordecai at gate and whispers to Mordecai, then bows as he talks)*

Mordecai: Tell her this ... "Just because you are in the king's house, you will not escape death. If you remain quiet, you and your entire family will die. Who knows, maybe God has put you in this royal position for such a time as this." *(Hathach nods and returns up steps to Esther and whispers to her)*

Esther: He is right, of course. Tell him that I will go to the king. If I die, I die ...

Narrator: *(Esther crosses over to center stage and bows in front of throne)* So Esther humbly approached the king and was offered the royal scepter. *(King holds out scepter and she touches tip)*

King: What is it, Queen Esther?

Esther: If it pleases you, I wish for you and Haman to come to a banquet which I will prepare for you today.

King: It would be our pleasure. *(Esther exits)* She sure is better than my last wife, eh?

Narrator: At the banquet, Esther asked the King and Haman to come to another banquet the next night. Afterward, Haman went home to build a gallows to hang Mordecai while the king read through his royal annals and found that Mordecai had once saved his life but had never been properly rewarded. The next morning, he sent for Haman.

King: *(Haman enters and sits down next to King)* Haman, what should I do to honor a man that has done a great thing for me?

Haman: Oh, King, you noticed! Why, put me, I mean him, in your robe, lead him through town on your horse, and shout to everyone that he is greatly honored.

King: Perfect. Go get Mordecai, give him my robe and horse, and you can escort him through town shouting his praises. *(Haman, looking sick, exits)*

Narrator: Things only got worse for Haman at the Queen's feast. *(Esther and Hathach bring in table. Haman enters. King, Esther, and Haman sit down at table and begin to eat)*

King: Now, Esther, tell me your wish so that I might grant it ...

Esther: *(Getting up from chair to kneel in front of King)* Grant me my life, O king, for my people and I are to be slaughtered at the end of the year.

King: What? Where is the man that would do such a thing?

Esther: Sitting right next to you. Haman urged you to decree that all Jews should be killed at the end of the year.

King: I must go out to the garden to think. Come on, Zethar. *(King and Zethar walk left stage and stand whispering together. Esther walks over to sitting room and lays down. Haman follows her and sits on her bed, begging for forgiveness)*

76

Narrator: *(King and Zethar enter sitting room)* When the King returned to find Haman in his wife's bed, he had him hanged that night on the very gallows Haman had built to hang Mordecai.

King: *(Walks center stage)* As I *am* the king, I decree that Mordecai will be my new advisor. *(Mordecai walks up steps stands next to King. Esther stands on other side)* But what do I about my decree to kill the Jews? I can't undo my first order!

Mordecai: If it please the king, allow the Jews to defend themselves against any attackers.

King: Great idea. Write the edict immediately and seal it with my ring.

Narrator: So the Jews were not destroyed as Haman had plotted. Instead, Queen Esther decreed that they should celebrate the survival of their people with the Festival of Purim, which is still observed today. As for Mordecai, he made many wise decisions for Persia, and earned the respect of many while always sticking up for the rights of his people.

Vocabulary
eunuch: an advisor / government official who was castrated to prevent him from having children who might rebel and try to establish dynasties of their own

harem: a separate building by the palace where the king's young virgins lived

annals: court journals

scepter: staff or rod

Discussion Questions

1. What choice did Queen Vashti make in this story? What were the consequences? Why do you think she refused to come to the king?

2. What choice did Esther make in this story? What were the consequences?

3. Describe King Xerxes. Have you ever worked with anyone like him? What are the advantages? Disadvantages?

4. Why did Esther and Mordecai keep the fact that she was Jewish a secret?

5. Mordecai thought that Esther was placed in her royal position to save her people. Do you believe that God places people in positions for certain purposes? Give examples.

Related Activities

1. Make a royal scepter. Take a paper towel roll and cover it with aluminum foil or sticky paper. Then glue or color gems onto it.

2. Look up the description of Xerxes' palace in Esther 1:6-7. Illustrate what the palace might have looked like.

3. Design a royal looking goblet.

4. Read about the beauty treatments and regulations for the harem in Esther 2:12-13. Draw a picture or cartoon of what you think living in a harem would be like, including conversation between the girls.

5. Read Esther 9:12-14 and Esther 9:16 to find out how many people the Jews killed on the thirteenth and fourteenth days of

Adar. Add these numbers up. How might things have been different if Mordecai and Esther had not influenced the king?

6. Add Character(s), Choice(s), Consequence(s), and Message Learned to your Bible Chart.

Strangers In A Strange Land: The Story Of Daniel And His Friends

A play based on Daniel 1-6

This one-act play is designed to be flexible. It can be read and discussed without using stage directions, or presented with props and costumes.

Scene: The Narrator stands at the lectern or stage left. There is a table in front of the lectern with fast food bags on it and four chairs around it. The furnace scene takes place center stage, and the lion's den right stage. Nebuchadnezzar and Ashpenaz are standing center stage in front of the furnace (fire) as the play begins.

Props: Cardboard fire for furnace, table, fast food bags and cups, 4 carrot sticks, trophy with athletic figure on it, red streamers cut into strips (fire), portable tent or blanket draped over coat rack, easel, or table set on side for lion's den

Sound Effects: Optional piano, organ, trumpet, or kazoo fanfare as noted in script. Audience participation meows and growls, per script.

Characters:
One actor/actress could easily play Astrologer and Guard, and another the Townsperson and Satrap, as these parts are small.
Narrator — reader
Ashpenaz — Chief of Court Officials
Daniel — lion-hearted, righteous prophet
Shadrach — Daniel's Hebrew friend
Mesach — Friend 2
Abednego — Friend 3

Nebuchadnezzar — (neb-uh-kud-NEZ-zer), Ruler of Babylon who had just defeated Jerusalem

Astrologer — respected advisor to the king

Townsperson — non-speaking

Guard — non-speaker with an attitude

Angel — non-speaker who frolics with three friends in furnace and disappears

Satrap — jealous royal administrator. Must be able to wrestle stuffed kitty and lose

King Darius — third king whom Daniel served. Others were Nebuchadnezzar, Belshazzar, and Cyrus

Time: about 605-535 B.C.

Costumes: Biblical tunics or robes for the four Friends, Astrologer, Townsperson, Satrap; Kings have royal robes and crowns; Angel is in white robe with halo and optional wings; Guard has plastic sword/ breastplate if available

---

Narrator: After Jerusalem was destroyed, four of its finest young men were taken into exile in Babylon by King Nebuchadnezzar to be trained to become court officials. This is their story.

Nebuchadnezzar: Ashpenaz, have you found me young men from Israel who are handsome, fit, and quick to learn?

Ashpenaz: Yes, my lord. They are Daniel, Shadrach, Mesach, and Abednego.

Nebuchadnezzar: Good. See to it that they learn the Babylonian language and writings, and that they are given food and wine from my table daily.

Ashpenaz: As you wish, sir.

Narrator: *(King and Ashpenaz exit. Ashpenaz returns right away bringing Daniel, Shadrach, Mesach, and Abednego back to stand center stage with him)* So, Daniel and his friends began training for the king's service.

Ashpenaz: *(Walking to table in front of stage which has fast food bags on it. Picks up food and offers to Daniel)* Daniel, you must eat the food given to you from the king's table. If you and your friends become too skinny, the king will have my head.

Daniel: Please, many of your meats are against our religion. Test us for ten days, giving us nothing but veggies to eat and water to drink. Then compare our looks with the guys who have eaten the royal food. Let's get started on our healthy regimen, boys. *(Daniel whips out four carrot sticks, and all four bite at once, crunching zestily. Ashpenaz sits down at table)*

Narrator: Ten days passed. *(Daniel and Friends sit down at table with Ashpenaz)*

Ashpenaz: Wow, Daniel! After ten days without royal food or wine, you actually look healthier than the others who feasted. *(Four Friends nod and smile. They flex muscles as they exit with Asphenaz)*

Narrator: So the first recorded vegetarians kept to their own simple diets and worshiped their God. After they entered the king's service, they were ten times wiser than any of his magicians. Now one day King Nebuchadnezzar had a golden statue made which was ninety feet high and nine feet wide. *(Nebuchadnezzar enters center stage carrying trophy with golden figure on it, followed by Townsperson, Astrologer, Shadrach, Mesach, and Abednego)* That's ninety feet high and nine feet wide?

Nebuchadnezzar: *(Shrugs shoulders)* What do you expect? This is a low-budget production! *(Holds trophy high above head)*

Narrator: At the dedication ceremony, all people were to worship it or be thrown into a fiery furnace. *(Optional fanfare. Townsperson, all others fall to knees to worship trophy except Shadrach, Mesach, and Abednego)*

Astrologer: Fair king, these three men — who have *top* government positions — have not fallen to their knees. Why do they ignore your law?

Nebuchadnezzar: Shadrach, why don't you worship my statue?

Shadrach: No idols for me. I worship only my God.

Nebuchadnezzar: You do realize, of course, that you will be thrown into a blazing furnace for disobeying?

Mesach: Fire away. If we are thrown into the furnace, our God can save us.

Abednego: But even if God chose not to, we would still never serve your gods.

Nebuchadnezzar: Heat the furnace seven times hotter than usual. I want the strongest guard in the palace to tie them up and throw them into the fire. *(Crowd stands back and kneels. Guard pushes three Friends toward cardboard fire and throws strands of red streamers on them)*

Narrator: So Shadrach, Mesach, and Abednego were pitched into the furnace. *(Angel enters and all four have a pretend game of volleyball with streamers as they're tossed on top of them)*

Nebuchadnezzar: Fools! They're toast. Wait a minute. Why do I see *four* men walking around the fire? Where did the fourth one come from, anyway? He looks like the son of the gods! They sure don't seem to be bothered by the heat. Men, come out! *(Angel disappears / hides behind fire or lectern. Shadrach, Mesach, and Abednego walk out in front of stage area)*

Narrator: The three came out of the fire, with not a burn on their bodies or hair out of place. *(Friends surround King Nebuchadnezzar, looking down on him as he cowers a bit)*

Nebuchadnezzar: *(Laughs nervously)* Doesn't it just *fry you* when a good joke falls flat? *(Three Friends raise eyebrows and roll eyes)* Hm-m-m. Well, you three obviously have a direct connection to a very powerful God. *(To Townspeople)* I decree that anyone who says anything against their God will be cut into pieces and find his/her home turned to serious rubble. *(Nebudchadnezzar throws arm around Shadrach and keeps talking as everyone on stage but narrator exits)* By the way, I'm giving you three *big* promotions.

Narrator: The three Jewish men and Daniel continued to worship their own God and were given even higher government positions when Darius became king. Daniel was given a purple robe, gold chain, and made number 3 man, making some at the palace more jealous than ever.

Satrap: *(King Darius, Satrap, and Guard enter and stand center stage)* Oh, King. Live for ever. Not everyone honors your greatness as I do. Some worship their own gods over you. *(Daniel enters, kneels right stage, hands folded and head bowed in prayer)*

King Darius: They do? Well, write up a decree or something for me, would you?

Satrap: Yes, sire. *(Clears throat. Optional fanfare)* On behalf of his majesty, I decree that for one month, no man may pray to any god except King Darius or he will be thrown into the lions' den. A-hem. Good King, I don't mean to be a Babblin'-onian, but look in Daniel's window. He prays to his own God and ignores your law. *(Gestures toward Daniel kneeling in prayer)*

King Darius: Since I can't change my decree, I can only hope that Daniel's God whom he prays to regularly will rescue him.

Narrator: The guard threw Daniel into the lions' den. *(Guard pushes Daniel into the den) (Speaking directly to audience)* Audience, this is the part of the story where I need your help. As Darius opens the door to the lions' den, I need you to purr and meow like a kitten ... The next morning, King Darius came to check on Daniel.

King Darius: *(Walking to right stage)* Daniel, has your God rescued you? *(Darius opens door to lions' den. Audience makes sound of purring kitten. Daniel walks out)*

Daniel: Bye, kitty. *(Bowing to King)* O king, live forever. My God sent his angel and shut the mouths of the lions. They have not hurt me, for I have done no wrong.

King Darius: There's no mark on you because you trusted in your God. But you have been falsely accused, so the men who plotted against you must be thrown to the lions in your place — along with their wives and children.

Narrator: *(To audience)* I need your help again. When the door opens to the lions' den this time, I need you to growl and roar like ferocious lions. *(Guard opens door of den and throws Satrap in. Audience growls and roars)* The wicked man was attacked before he even reached the floor of the den. *(Satrap disappears in den, screams, never comes out)* Some say that's what he got for *ly-in'*!

King Darius: My loyal subjects, I have a decree. *(Optional fanfare)* Everyone in the kingdom must respect Daniel's God, for twice he has rescued Daniel and his friends from impossible situations.

Discussion Questions
1. What choices did Daniel and his three friends make?

2. How did God reward them?

3. Do you think it would be hard to stick to your own ways if you were moved away from your family to a country with a different language, food, religion, and customs?

4. Why were the four Jewish men so respected in a foreign land?

5. How do the Babylonian forms of punishment compare with ours today?

Related Activities
1. Make props for the play:
   a. Paint a fire on cardboard for the furnace. Make optional sign: "Caution: Hot Surface."
   b. Cut red streamers into strips for the fire.
   c. Construct lions' den by draping blanket over easel, table turned on side, or coat stands, etc. Make sure flap can be lifted in front as a door. May make optional sign: "Lions' Den: Enter at Your Own Risk."
   d. Write the name of a biblical sounding fast food restaurant on a paper bag, e.g., McDaniels, Babylonian Burger Boy, or Burger Empire.

2. Present the play to younger children.
   a. Afterward, let them role play the lions in the den with Daniel, and the lions in the den with the Satrap.
   b. Sing with them all of the verses of "Who Did Swallow Jonah?" (*Wee Sing Bible Songs* by Beall and Nipp, Price/ Stern/Sloan, 1986).

3. Fill in your choice chart with Bible Character(s), Choice(s), Consequences, and Message Learned.

4. Create a time line on a long piece of paper, marking the approximate time each Bible character you've studied lived.

5. Plan and eat a vegetarian meal or snack. You can name foods as per story if you wish ... (e.g., Abednego's Apples, Daniel's Dip, Mesach's Multi-grain Muffins, Guard's Grapes, Lion's Mane Mandarin Oranges, Asphenaz's Phruit Punch, etc.).

The Lord's Servant: The Story Of Mary

A play based on the book of Luke

This play can be used as a reading to spark discussion or performed with simple props. It is designed in one act, though the action continues through several settings. A baby angel or sheep walking across the front of the stage with a sign designates a change in setting. A sanctuary or auditorium with stairs or different levels would be perfect for this production.

Scenes: Sign Carrier carries sign with town name across front of the sanctuary to signal change of setting: Nazareth, Judea, Bethlehem, Jerusalem, Nazareth, Jerusalem

Props: Carpenter's apron with measuring tape and awl, 2x4 piece of wood, manger, baby doll, blanket, cross (use one already hanging in church, if possible)

Sound Effects: Barn animal sounds: cattle lowing, sheep baa-ing

Characters:

Sign Carrier — non-speaking Angel or Sheep / may be very young child who is led by an older Angel or Shepherd, or even pulled in a wagon

Mary — thoughtful, obedient servant / mother of Jesus

Elizabeth — Mary's older cousin

Gabriel — angel of the Lord

Zechariah — non-speaking, husband of Elizabeth

Joseph — a very precise carpenter, Mary's husband

Sheep — Jesus' roommate (could be very young child)

Cow — Friend of the family's (could be very young child)

Shepherd 1 — first to see the Babe
Shepherd 2 — Bethlehem visitor
Simeon — old man in the temple
Anna — old woman in the temple
Jesus — non-speaking, son of God as older boy/man

Time: about 6 B.C. until 17 A.D.

Costumes: Angel (white robe, wings, halo) or Sheep (fleecy ears, white sweats) costume for Sign Carrier; biblical robes for Mary, Elizabeth, Zechariah, and Jesus; white robe with wings for Gabriel, halo; biblical robe with carpenter's apron for Joseph; biblical robes with optional beard for Simeon and white hair for Anna; fleecy headgear with white sweats for Sheep; hat with horns and brown sweats for Cow; biblical robes with optional crooks and stuffed sheep for Shepherds

---

Mary: *(Standing center stage, in front of steps)* I had the privilege of knowing Jesus longer than anyone else on earth. I saw him come into the world, and I watched him go out. My name is Mary, and this is my story ... I was living in Nazareth in Galilee.

Sign Carrier: *(Walks through front of church with sign that says "Nazareth," down side aisle, and out door)*

Mary: I was engaged to a *stud-ly* carpenter named Joseph.

Joseph: *(Enters, waves hello, and proceeds to pull out measuring tape and measure height of lectern, step, and length of front pew)*

Mary: Joseph, do you mind?

Joseph: *(Snaps tape shut)* Oh, sorry, Mary. Just one more measurement to check with the blueprint ... *(Measures from nearest pew out the door as he exits)*

Mary: *(Shaking her head)* My life was moving along very nicely when I got my first news flash that I was going to follow God's plan, not my own!

Gabriel: *(Enters and stands on higher level such as chair, lectern, or choir loft — calling down to Mary)* Greetings, O favored one. The Lord is with you.

Mary: What do you mean, "favored one"?

Gabriel: Don't be afraid, Mary. You have found favor with God. He has chosen you to carry and give birth to a son whom you are to name Jesus. Jesus will be the Son of the Most High, and will reign over the house of Jacob forever.

Mary: Wait a minute. I'm confused about the "give birth to a son" part. I'm a virgin.

Gabriel: The Holy Spirit will come upon you and overshadow you. And the holy one which will be born will be called the Son of God. Just so you know that nothing is impossible for God, your cousin, Elizabeth, who everyone thought was too old ever to have children is already six months pregnant.

Mary: *(Humbly)* I am the Lord's servant. May it be as you have said. *(Gabriel leaves)* Elizabeth, pregnant? I've got to hustle my bustle over to see her in Judea.

Sign Carrier: *(Walks through front of sanctuary with sign saying "Judea," down side aisle, and out door. Mary walks down steps and circles back up to center stage. Elizabeth enters and greets Mary with a hug)*

Mary: Hello, cousin. How's my little mother-to-be?

Elizabeth: When you spoke just now, the baby inside me jumped at your voice, and I'm filled with the Holy Spirit. I know that you're blessed, Mary. In fact, I feel privileged to have the mother of my Lord come for a visit.

Mary: That's funny. My baby just jostled for joy inside of me, too. Their first meeting — and they haven't even been born. Bless you for believing what the Lord has said. I was beginning to think it was all just a dream. Oh, hello, Zechariah. Thank you for taking me into your home.

Zechariah: *(Waves hello)*

Mary: What's the matter, cat got your tongue?

Elizabeth: No, more like an angel. He can't speak — ever since he didn't believe the good news that we were going to have a baby when the angel Gabriel told him in a vision. All he does is make signs.

Mary: Let me stay and help you. It can't be easy getting ready for a baby at your age, cousin. *(Mary puts arm around Elizabeth and the two walk down center aisle, around pews, and back up center stage, whispering earnestly about their babies)* Time passed quickly, and soon I had to get back home. *(Elizabeth and Mary hug. Mary pats Elizabeth's belly, then Elizabeth exits)*

Sign Carrier: *(Walks through front of church with "Nazareth" sign, down side aisle, out door. Mary walks down steps, around a few pews, and back up steps, center stage. Joseph enters with 2x4 and awl)*

Mary: Elizabeth wrote to tell me she'd had her baby. They named him John. Zechariah finally got his voice back and praised the Lord, for he knew that John would be a great prophet who would prepare the way for the Lord. I was praising the Lord myself, for he helped my doubting fiancé, Joseph, understand that the baby I was carrying was God's Son. In the end, my classy carpenter *showed his timber (Joseph holds up 2x4)* when he accepted *awl. (Joseph holds up awl)*

Joseph: (*Whips out measuring tape, and measures around Mary's stomach*)

Mary: Joseph, will you stop measuring things!

Joseph: Sorry, Mary. I know that it will be hard for you to travel with the baby due soon, but we must go to Bethlehem to register, since that is the town of my ancestor, David.

Sign Carrier: (*Walks through front of church with "Bethlehem" sign, down side aisle, out door. Shepherds enter and stand out in fields tending sheep, to left of stage, in front of steps*)

Mary: In Bethlehem, life was crazy. There was no room for us at the inn, so we found a nice, *stable* place to stay. (*Mary and Joseph walk down steps, around a block of pews and back up steps to center stage. Joseph places manger with baby in it between them, and he and Mary kneel by manger. Cow and Sheep join them*) Under the watchful eye of a curious cow and some fleecy sheep, on a bed of sweet-smelling hay, I had my firstborn son, Jesus. (*Takes baby from manger and cradles him*) I didn't worry that we had no fancy nursery or state-of-the-art baby wipes. It was the happiest night of my entire life. (*Sound effects — animals make barnyard noises*)

Joseph: Here, Mary. Let me hold the little *wood-shaver*. (*Whips out measuring tape and measures length of child*)

Mary: Joseph, you're doing it again!

Joseph: Nineteen inches. Write that down in his baby book. Okay, okay, I'll stop. (*Snaps tape shut*) I'll just wrap him in these cloths (*Wraps in blanket*), and we'll lay him in the manger. What are you smiling about now?

Mary: I was just thinking, if Jesus is sloppy or slams the door a lot, we'll never be able to ask him if he was *born in a barn*, because he really was!

Cow: That baby's coo is *mooo*-sic to my ears.

Sheep: Just look at the little lambkin, *baaaa*-sking in moonlight.

Mary: Just then, some shepherds came hurrying up, and fell on their knees before us.

Shepherd 1: *(Shepherds enter from left stage, walk up steps, and kneel in front of manger)* We've found you.

Sheep: Baaaaaaa!

Shepherd 2: Just as the angel said — the babe is wrapped in cloths and lying in the manger. He is Christ the Lord.

Shepherd 1: "Glory be to God in the highest, and on earth peace to men on whom his favor rests."

Shepherd 2: Let's go now and tell everyone we know. Praise the Lord, Christ is born!

Mary: These were the first treasures in the scrapbook of my heart, but they wouldn't be the last. When he was eight days old, we officially named the baby Jesus as the angel had told me, and took him to Jerusalem to be circumcised.

Sign Carrier: *(Walks through front of church with "Jerusalem" sign, down side aisle, and out door. Shepherds and Animals exit, taking manger with them. Mary and Joseph with baby walk down steps, and circle back up steps to center stage where Simeon and Anna are waiting)*

Mary: There, a faithful man named Simeon saw us. He took Jesus into his arms, saying ...

Simeon: *(Takes baby, lays hand on Mary's shoulder. Speaks in quivering voice)* Bless you, Mary, mother of Jesus. This child will cause many to rise and fall in Israel and many to reveal the thoughts in their hearts. And a sword will pierce your own soul, too.

Mary: While I was still pondering Simeon's words, a very old widow name Anna came up to us.

Anna: *(Takes baby from Simeon, who steps back. Anna kneels with baby and addresses audience)* Thank you, Lord, for this child. People of the temple, do you know that this is the one the prophets have foretold? The one who has come to save Jerusalem?

Mary: Then we went back to Nazareth in Galilee where Jesus grew and became strong, wise, and filled with the grace of God. *(Anna and Simeon exit. Mary and Joseph travel down steps and circle back up center stage. Along the way, they lay baby down, and older Jesus joins them. Entire Cast assembles on steps in groups of two or three)*

Sign Carrier: *(As Mary and Joseph are circling around, Sign Carrier walks across front of church with "Nazareth" sign down side aisle, and out door)*

Mary: Elizabeth's son, John the Baptist, lived up to his father's words, and told everyone about the coming of Jesus. Then Jesus began his ministry at age thirty. He didn't beat around the burning bush, but taught people how to love each other and find eternal life. *(Jesus walks among Cast Members. Some act sick, crippled, or blind. When he touches them, they are healed. Jesus pantomimes telling stories to others, who listen attentively)* For three years, he healed many who were sick, and always spoke up for the weak and the poor. Though many loved him, the religious leaders hated him because he criticized their silly laws and pompous ways. They rejected my son, mocked him, and beat him. *(Four Cast Members pantomime beating, nailing Jesus to cross)* Finally, they put him to death on a cross. *(Jesus stands in front of cross with arms outstretched, hangs head. Cast watches silently. Some cry,* *some kneel. Four who beat him laugh and exit)* Seeing my son hanging lifeless on the cross, the words of the old man in the temple rang in my ears ...

Simeon: *(Enters, speaks as a memory from lectern above)* ... And a sword will pierce your own soul, too.

Mary: Would I do it again if God asked me? *(Nods yes)* Of course, for I am, as always, the Lord's servant. *(Bows head obediently)*

Discussion Questions
1. What choice did Mary make in this skit?

2. What were the consequences of her choice?

3. How does Mary's acceptance of unbelievable news in her life compare to Zechariah's? What were the consequences of Zechariah's lack of belief?

4. How did Joseph show that he had faith?

5. Have your own plans for your life ever been totally changed due to circumstances beyond your control? Did you fight the change, accept it obediently, or do something in between? Was the change for the better or worse?

6. Why do you think God chose Mary to be Jesus' mother?

Related Activities
1. Design and build a manger to use as a prop.

2. Read Matthew 1:18-22 to find out more about Joseph's feelings concerning the big change in his life and Mary's.

3. Read Matthew 3:1-15 to find out how John the Baptist is described. Draw a picture or cartoon of him in the desert.

4. Listen to and sing John the Baptist's song, "Prepare Ye," from the musical *Godspell.* For whom does he want the people to prepare?

5. Make a card for your own mom telling her how much you appreciate her.

6. Add Mary's, Joseph's, and Zechariah's Character(s), Choice(s), Consequence(s), and Message Learned to your class chart.

Jesus:
The Unselfish King

A play based on Luke 22-24

This play is designed to be read using no props or scenery, or performed using simple effects. It works best on a stage with two levels connected by steps.

Scenes: The Narrator stands at lectern or off stage with microphone. Center stage is Garden of Gethsemane and later courts where Jesus is tried. A ladder stands next to the altar; down steps in front of center stage is courtyard where Peter denies Jesus; right stage in front of steps is upper room with two stools; right stage second level is where Jesus stands to wait for trial, and later is crucified. Left stage in front of steps is tomb.

Props: Optional bread and wine; cross, hammer, nail, board; sign that says, "This is the King of the Jews"; optional tomb, stone, white cloths; ladder

Sound Effects: (Optional) Rooster crowing three times, hammer striking nail four times

Characters:
Narrator — reader
Jesus — the unselfish king
Peter — well-meaning but clueless disciple
Servant — girl who accuses Peter
Man 1 — accuses Peter
Man 2 — accuses Peter
Guard — non-speaking
Priest — accuses Jesus

Pilate — leader of Roman territory
Simon of Cyrene — carries Jesus' cross, non-speaking
Soldier — mocks Jesus
Centurion — Roman officer who believes
Woman — Jesus' friend who wants to help bury him
Angel — talks to women at tomb

Time: about 6 B.C. until 30 A.D.

Costumes: Biblical robes, sashes, headpieces, sandals for Jesus, Peter, Servant Girl, Men, Simon, Woman. Jesus will be wearing raggedy wrap underneath for crucifixion, then change to white robe for resurrection. Guard and Soldier will wear breastplates, armbands, or carry fake swords; Priest will wear light robe and carry scroll; Pilate and Centurion will have royal looking material draped over one arm, and sandals with leather strips that lace up legs. Angel will wear white robe.

Narrator: This is the story of a very unusual king named Jesus. He wasn't interested in gold trappings or a huge empire, but in teaching how to live and love. Now Jesus was God's son, and not afraid to say it. He was loved and hated in his time, for though he healed and taught many, he also made strong statements that went against popular beliefs and made the Jewish religious leaders look bad. One night, as they broke bread and drank wine, Jesus tried to prepare his twelve faithful followers for his upcoming death.

Jesus: *(Sitting on stool with Peter in front of steps right stage. Optional props bread, wine)* Peter, Satan will try to crush you like so many grains of wheat, so I've prayed that your faith won't fail. In fact, I know that you'll come back to me and be a source of strength to others. That's why I changed your name from Simon to Peter — "the rock."

Peter: Are you kidding? Lord, I'd *die* for you.

Jesus: I tell you, Peter, before the rooster crows this morning, you will deny knowing me three times.

Narrator: Next they all went to pray at the Mount of Olives. *(Jesus and Peter walk up steps, center stage)*

Peter: Wow, I'm really exhausted. All that worry, wine, and this night air is making me so ... Z-zzzzzzzzzz. *(Curls up and goes to sleep)*

Narrator: While his disciples snored away, Jesus talked to God. *(Jesus is on knees, praying)*

Jesus: Father, I don't want to die. Can we change the plan?

Narrator: Jesus prayed so hard that he was dripping sweat like blood.

Jesus: *(Nodding head, speaking heavenward)* Of course, I'll do it *Thy* way, not *my* way.

Narrator: An angel came and gave him strength, and finally he was ready to face his death. *(Jesus gets up, puts his hand on Peter's shoulder)*

Jesus: What — you're all sleeping? You guys should be praying that you don't fall into temptation.

Narrator: At that moment, a crowd came up to them. One of his twelve disciples, Judas, came up and kissed him. *(Guard, Servant Girl, Man 1 and Man 2 and stand in semicircle around Jesus)*

Jesus: Judas, you're betraying me with a kiss?

Narrator: Jesus knew that Judas hadn't kissed him out of respect, but was really showing the guards who to arrest. Then he was led to the house of the high priest to be tried in the middle of the night, since the religious leaders knew that Jesus' fans would never let him be arrested in broad daylight. *(Guard walks Jesus around pews and back up steps right stage where Jesus stands with hands bound behind back as if being questioned. Servant, Men, and Peter walk down steps; sit in semicircle around pretend fire center stage)* Peter followed at a distance, sitting down at a fire in the courtyard during the questioning. A servant girl next to Peter looked closely at his face.

Servant: You were with him.

Peter: Woman, I don't know him.

Man 1: She's right. You're one of them.

Peter: You're wrong.

Man 2: I'm sure of it, too. You're a Galilean. You were with him.

Peter: What are you talking about? *(Shouts) I don't know him!*

Narrator: Just then, the rooster crowed and Jesus turned and looked straight at him. *(Jesus turns and looks at Peter. Peter stands and looks at Jesus)* Peter remembered Jesus' words, "... before the rooster crows this morning you will deny knowing me three times," and ran outside sobbing bitter tears. Meanwhile, the guards began beating Jesus and mocking him.

Narrator: *(Guard, Jesus, Crowd walk center stage where Priest is standing)* As day was breaking, the council of elders and all of the important Jewish leaders and teachers tried to come up with a reason to arrest him.

Priest: Are you the Son of God?

Jesus: You are right in saying that I am.

Priest: Blasphemy!

Narrator: The council made up their minds. They took Jesus to Pilate, who was the Roman governor of the area. He passed the buck to Herod who took care of Galilean matters, but Herod could find no basis for charging Jesus and sent him back to Pilate. *(Pilate enters)*

Pilate: He doesn't deserve to die. How about if I just punish him? Then I'll let him go.

Man 1: Crucify him! Crucify him!

Pilate: That seems harsh. What crime has he committed?

Narrator: Pilate was not too popular with his big bosses in Rome, and having the Jews complain about his rule in Judea would not help his reputation, so he finally gave up.

    The whole crowd had really whipped themselves into a frenzy by now. The Roman guards led Jesus away. *(Jesus pulls off outer robe and is wearing shabby wrap around waist)* He had been beaten so badly that he couldn't carry his own cross, so Simon from Cyrene carried it for him. Some of the women who followed were wailing loudly. *(Simon carries cross, Jesus crawls, Crowd follows down steps and back up right stage where Jesus is nailed to cross. Women are crying)* Jesus was nailed to the cross between two other criminals in a place called the Skull. *(Guard pantomimes nailing Jesus to cross. Optional sound effects: hammer hitting nail four times. Jesus stands with arms straight out as if nailed to cross)*

Jesus: Father, forgive them, for they don't know what they're doing!

Soldier: Yeah, yeah. Save it, King. Okay, let's draw straws. The shortest one gets his sandals. And here, I made a sign for your majesty. It says, "This is the King of the Jews," so none of your loyal subjects will forget you. *(Laughs mockingly and places sign at top of cross)*

Narrator: At the sixth hour, darkness came over the whole land. *(Lights go out)* The sun stopped shining, and the curtain of the Temple through which only the priests could enter the Most Holy Place was torn in two. Jesus called out loudly.

Jesus: Father, into your hands I commit my spirit.

Narrator: And he breathed his last. *(Jesus hangs head)*

Centurion: *(Looking fearfully at darkness all around)* I'm a Roman, and even I can see that this was a righteous man. *(Jesus exits while lights are off. Changes into white robe)*

Narrator: Now, Joseph of Arimathea from the council had not agreed with their decision to kill Jesus. He took Jesus' body, wrapped it in linen cloth, and placed it in a tomb. The weeping women followed him to the tomb, but they couldn't prepare the body for burial because it was almost the sabbath. Early the next morning they came back to the tomb.

Woman: What's this? The stone has been rolled away. And ... there's *no body*!

Narrator: Suddenly two men appeared whose clothes gleamed like lightning.

Angel: Why do you look for the living among the dead? He's not here; he has risen! Remember in Galilee, Jesus told you that "... the Son of Man must be delivered into the hands of sinful men, be crucified, and on the third day be raised again."

Woman: I remember. We must hurry and tell the eleven disciples and the others. *(Quickly exits)*

Narrator: No one believed the women, thinking them hysterical. But Peter ran to the tomb. Bending over, he saw the strips of linen lying there, and went away wondering. *(Peter checks out tomb,* *walks down center aisle shaking head. Jesus, dressed in white robe, joins him)* Jesus in the flesh appeared to the disciples, letting them touch his hands and his feet so they would know he had really come back from the dead. *(Peter touches hands, feet, side)*

Peter: I finally get it. Everything came true as you said it would. *(Peter falls to his knees at Jesus' feet)*

Narrator: As Jesus lifted up his hands and blessed them, he was taken up into heaven. *(Jesus lifts hands to bless, walks down center aisle to altar, climbs ladder, and stands with arms outstretched)* And Peter and the other ten disciples finally understood what Jesus had been telling them for three years. Now they would spread the good news to all peoples about Jesus — the unselfish king.

Discussion Questions
1. What choice did Jesus make in the Garden? What were the consequences?

2. What choice did Peter make when he was accused of being Jesus' follower? What would you have done in his position?

3. In what ways might Peter have disappointed Jesus in this skit?

4. What made Peter and the disciples finally understand Jesus' message?

5. In what ways was Jesus unlike the typical king?

Related Activities
1. Make props and sound effects:
   a. Nail together two pieces of wood for cross.
   b. On cardboard, paint cave with big opening, and stone rolled away.

    c.   Tape record or practice rooster crow.

    d.   Tape or practice striking hammer for crucifixion scene.

2.   Read Luke 22:49-51 and Luke 23:39-43 to find examples of how Jesus was compassionate even during the biggest crisis of his life.

3.   Sing "Were You There" or "Lord Of The Dance" to see how closely these hymns follow the description of Jesus' death in the Bible.

4.   Read Luke 24:4-11 to find out more about the women who discovered the empty tomb. Now read John 20:14-18 to read a different account of the same event. Make a Venn diagram comparing what was the same and different about the two accounts. List events that happened only in Luke's account in the oval on the left, events that happened only in John's account in the oval on the right, and events that happened in both accounts in the middle where the two ovals intersect. (See following example.)

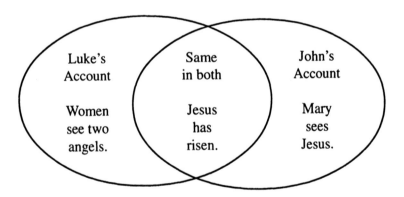

5.   Add Jesus' and Peter's names to your master chart of Character(s), Choice(s), Consequence(s), and Messages Learned.

CPSIA information can be obtained at www.ICGtesting.com
Printed in the USA
BVOW03s1113270813

329500BV00008B/162/P